THE WAR OF THE MIND

PRISON BY ANOTHER NAME

ECHE EGBUONU

AMAZON KDP

CONTENTS

PROLOGUE

I stood in the centre of my bedroom, flanked by furniture. The broken printer was nested neatly underneath the computer, but the room itself was a mess. My black plimsoles began to pace up and down the carpet, which had recovered from the recent water damage. My mother and brother were somewhere in the flat, and I couldn't help but wonder what they were thinking. The prodigal son had returned.

It must have been an hour or so before the sound of loud knocking on the door permeated the air. *It has to be them,* I thought. Who else would knock so obnoxiously? Within moments, three police officers strolled into my bedroom wearing green uniforms: two male and one female.

This was my fifth encounter with the metropolitan police in the last four weeks. Shortly after the officers entered, my brother and my friends also joined. They gathered near the door and kept a watchful eye, perhaps hoping to spot any foul play. For me, the days of compliance were over, and I was going to stand my ground. The thought of going back to the hospital gave me all the motivation I needed.

It was apparent from my body language that I wouldn't be complying with the request to be handcuffed. Flight wasn't an option, which left fighting as the only alternative. The officers soon ran out of patience as they understood the futility of reasoning with me. As the officers stepped towards me, I clenched my fist and tensed all of the muscles in my body. *Here we go,* I thought.

The officers tried to grab each of my arms, hoping to handcuff me, but I was as slippery as I was strong. We wrestled in the centre of my bedroom for what seemed like an eternity. In actuality, it was a minute or so. Failure was not an option for me, as the stakes were too high. They could have left me alone, but they violated my sacred space. We continued to dance violently and jostle. I had remained on my two feet and was putting up a solid resistance. My friends and brother watched worriedly from the corner of the bedroom; it looked like someone was recording, but I couldn't tell for sure.

There was no winner after the first round. We had reached a stalemate. For the officers, it appeared a change of strategy was needed. The female officer grabbed the yellow taser from the holster on her hip.

Two darts were fired from the taser into my abdomen with deadly precision. It was extraordinarily effective. In an instant, my legs gave way, and I immediately collapsed in a heap in the centre of my bedroom. The officers wasted no time and handcuffed me while I was immobilised.

Resistance, in this case, was futile, and it felt like the nightmare would never end. I scowled at my brother and friends as the police officers escorted me from my room and into the police car. I grew increasingly anxious as we drove to the mental health hospital.

CHAPTER ONE

REFLECTIONS

I didn't cry when I was born. I'm not sure why, but my best guess is that even back then, I didn't want to cause a scene and bring attention to myself.

Being out of sync is a consistent theme in my life with my poor eyesight serving as the earliest physical manifestation. One eye was long sighted and the other was short. The imbalance is so acute, it's the equivalent of having one foot as a size six and the other a size nine. The glasses corrected my vision but I couldn't help but feel like I was viewing life from a skewed perspective.

My grandmother suggested the name Echézona to my mother. In Igbo culture, the names of babies are often associated with God, and mine was no exception. It means "never forget God." I preferred the shortened version, splicing my name in two, choosing to be referred to as Eché.

I was born in Nigeria but I have spent the vast majority of my life in London. To say that my life was filled with adversity would be an exaggeration. The most significant danger that I faced happened prior to our move to the UK. When I was a toddler in

Nigeria, a particular illness was prevalent, which resulted in severe convulsions and often led to the death of very young children. I was afflicted with this condition and the attacks were frequent and aggressive. Fortunately for me, medicine was administered and ultimately, I lived.

My mother used to place me down on the floor as an infant, and I would sit there perfectly happy in my own space, no tears and no need for interaction. This same behaviour would manifest itself in a myriad of ways as I grew older. My fourth birthday party encapsulates this perfectly. Smiles were rife and the atmosphere was jovial as the house swarmed with children buzzing around, enjoying the festivities. My eyes dilated as I clutched onto my mother's leg with the force of a vice grip. I was terrified by the chaos that unfolded around me. Things would go from bad to worse as it was now time for the birthday boy to dance. This was truly the stuff of nightmares. First, I had to deal with this overload of sensory stimuli and now I had to contend with the additional pressure of the video camera and a sea of staring eyes. Even at that early age, it was apparent that I cared way too much about how others perceived me. The best I could muster was to wave my foot left to right repeatedly. I haven't held a birthday party since.

I grew up in a council estate in East London. The transition from analogue to digital was in full swing and I moved into the 21st century with excitement and great expectations. I didn't have to venture far to find friends as the estate was home to a range of characters and personalities. I lived on the same housing block as two individuals who would go on to become two of my closest friends. Fate brought us together; we had a common heritage, but ultimately, it was shared values and interests that connected us. Football was one of the activities that we bonded over. Thirty seconds away from my flat was what I consider the heart and soul of the estate. Some called it the Red Pitch but I preferred "The Cage." It was one of the few places where I could let my guard down and be myself. The pitch was situated below street level and so it felt like an underground bunker at times. Silhouettes and paintings of athletes from a wide array of fields decorated the walls. However, we only ever played football and basketball. If the walls could talk, they would describe hours upon hours of intense competition and social bonds being formed. There was safety in the cage; I made friends in the cage; but most importantly, I found freedom in the cage.

Of all my educational experiences, my time at primary school was the most intuitive. Beneath the fog of nostalgia is a period in which my creativity was encouraged. In my personal economy, self-esteem was scarce and the only thing that I could turn to for some source of validation was my studies. The praise from my parents and encouragement from my teachers was positively reinforcing and kept me working hard. My crowning achievement was being one of two students who were offered to sit the extension paper having achieved the highest grade on the standardised tests. Even though I didn't achieve the grade six in the end, I was still in exclusive territory.

I wasn't worried about fitting in, having learned early on to go my own way. That philosophy served me well, up until late in my adolescence. I built up a reputation as the mild-mannered, painfully shy child who often knew the answers but was too afraid to raise his hand. There was another side of me which only manifested when I was in the company of my closest childhood friend, Kenny. Even though we wore the same uniform, he somehow managed to make it distinct and cool, tapping into his endless cauldron of creativity. We listened to Michael Jackson tapes and made dodecahedrons out of plastic shapes, paying no mind to what the rest of the toddlers in our class were doing. Our capacity for mischief was unprecedented, and together, we were involved in all manner of shenanigans. We embraced our eccentricities and navigated primary and secondary education as misfits.

Year nine was the year that the privileges in school began to accumulate. We were now allowed to leave the school site and secure our own lunches. But what I was really anticipating was being able to use the school gym. About six of us stepped through the grey doors. My eyes immediately locked onto the bench press. Situated next to it were some treadmills, a rowing machine, and a handful of other machines. My ears perked up as we proceeded through the induction. First up was the bench press and my wrists naturally curled against the stainless steel barbell. The tension within my muscle was sensational, the perfect mix of pleasure and pain. It was love at first rep.

We rotated, each completing sets on the bench press. Everyone was more or less in the same range when it came to repetitions completed. And then up stepped Juan.

I waited with bated breath to see if he would beat my number of reps. Juan was short and stocky, blessed with a physique that commands attention. I internally counted his reps and time slowed down as he approached the seven reps I completed.

Six...seven...eight...nine...TEN...ELEVEN... TWELVE! He absolutely smashed me. The chorus of excitement and congratulations from the fellas was deafening.

'Bro, you killed it!' I said, with an artificial smile plastered across my face.

I went to an all-boys school in the heart of London. The term central foundation was certainly appropriate. My personality certainly crystallised there.

'Yo, Eché, are you coming, Angel? We're gonna meet some of the girls from EGA?'

'I got a dentist appointment, bro.'

I had no such appointment. But it was the first lie that came to mind and seemed plausible enough. The next time I was invited I gave a similar excuse, and before I knew it, the invitations stopped.

I quickly learned how to play the education game. Keep my head down and stay out of trouble. It had served me well in primary school, so why change a working system? I became a class prefect and was top set in all of my subjects. One of the few advantages of being painfully shy is that it makes it easy to develop a reputation as a teacher's pet. I caused them no grief in the classroom and would reap material benefits on occasion.

Non-uniform day. The bane of my existence. A chance for the coolest kids to temporarily retire the school uniform and demonstrate their flair for fashion, embarrassing us mere mortals. Hip hop fashion effortlessly flowed across the pond and shaped the trends in inner city London. Avirex and Akademiks were the top brands at the time and I watched in astonishment when one of my peers was spotted in the same jacket that was seen in a myriad of rap videos. In year 10, I managed to get my hands on what was most probably a fake set of Akademiks tracksuit and hoody. I wore it to non-uniform day but couldn't pull it off. Thank God for school uniforms. I couldn't imagine having to repeat this struggle every day of the week.

Richard for me was the coolest kid in the whole school. He had a Colgate smile, was athletic, and was fantastically charismatic.

Through the grapevine, I heard that dozens of students were planning to go to another school during the lunch break to settle some inter-school rivalry. Richard of all people pleaded for me to join them.

'Eché, we're leaving in 15 minutes, are you rolling?'

'Why is everyone going to the school?'

'Cause they roughed up John last week.'

'I'm gonna chill here, bro.'

'Are you sure? Tyrone, Tobi, Jerome, everyone's rolling.'

'I'm not involved,' I replied, making sure to avoid any eye contact.

I'm happy right here playing Connect 4.

The school was a ghost town at lunch. Half-empty. The lads flocked back into school at the end of lunchtime, sweating and telling stories of police encounters. My friends mentioned how they had enough numbers to surround the outside of the rival school.

There I was, your prototypical introvert, but the extreme shyness prevented me from being myself consistently. Around my close friends, namely those that I grew up with, I could be me. There was no fear of judgement and my quirky side was able to express itself freely. However, in uncertain environments with new people, I would retreat further into my shell. I very seldom initiated conversations. My teachers and most of my classmates only saw a diluted version of me. It was a very crippling form of social anxiety. Being both introverted and painfully shy felt like a curse in an extrovert's world.

College was merely a stepping-stone to university. I wasn't certain of what I wanted to do career-wise but there was no doubt that I'd be reading business management at university. I saw myself in a three piece suit, with a suitcase in hand. The only choice would be Liverpool Street or Canary Wharf in terms of where I work.

College is a two year experience, so compared to primary and secondary school, it's very short lived. I navigated college like a ghost, struggling to make an impression. I was on good terms with my classmates but we didn't really hang out outside of lessons. Fortunately for me, at least a dozen people from secondary school also attended, as well as my best friend, Gabriel.

Gabriel lived one floor above me and we would usually walk to college together. But some days our timetables differed and I would make the journey alone. On a lovely spring day, I walked to college with the goal of asking out one of my classmates.

I scanned my ID and entered the building. My heart fluttered. The first period was 10 minutes away, and so a sea of students were waiting in the lobby. I almost strained my neck as I looked left and right, desperately seeking a familiar face. Time was running out. *How can I not know anybody in this lobby? Even a semi-acquaintance would be good enough, I would happily be the third wheel right now.* But I failed to find anybody, so I had to abort the mission. I found the nearest door and fled the scene. *Let me just wait outside of the classroom.*

Nicole from my politics class was the total package. She was smart, beautiful, and having appeared in some films and TV shows, was probably the most famous person I knew. Lord knows what possessed me the day that I asked her out. My shoulders slouched and I struggled to make eye contact, but with great strain, the words eventually tumbled out of my mouth. The rejection was quick and painless, or so I thought. The next day, I was habitually scrolling through my Facebook feed when I spotted a post by Nicole. As I read each word, I began to feel smaller and smaller. By the end of the post, I was microscopic. She basically described the scenario in which I asked her out and explained how much of a loser I was for even attempting it. She did everything but name me. And thank God she didn't. I wouldn't have been able to return to college if my name was included in that Facebook post.

Attending university was a major landmark for me and the occasion was made better by my friends helping me to move in. My big brother rented a van and drove me and three of my friends down to Birmingham. We had to harness our latent Tetris abilities to make my belongings and all four of us fit in the same van.

When I narrowed my university choices to Birmingham and Loughborough, I went for the less risky option and opted for Aston University. Birmingham has been deemed the "second city" after London, and I felt that it would be easier to adapt to another urban setting as opposed to the more suburban Loughborough.

The prospect of independent living frightened me as much as it excited me. I would be hundreds of miles away from my friends and family, which could be both a blessing and a curse. Was I up to the task? Spending those precious hours with family and friends helped alleviate some of the anxiety I felt. We met some of the other students who were also staying in the student accommodation. The residence halls were a bit dilapidated, but it was the cheapest option. Living on campus certainly had its benefits. The impact of missed alarms could be mitigated by the lecture theatres being a few minutes away. The atmosphere in the kitchen was filled with optimism and the drinks that we shared marked what would hopefully be the beginning of a memorable four years. The aroma of vodka and lemonade saturated the air. My brother glanced at his phone and let me know that it was time for them to go. As I thanked them for making this journey with me, the smile on my face changed from genuine to mechanical. It slowly dawned on me that for the next four years, I'd be hundreds of miles away from my best friends and brother. My left hand waved goodbye and I stood there helplessly watching my support network and emotional refuge drive back to London.

I was the top student in primary school, and so naturally, I thought I was pretty smart. But then I went to secondary school and met William. He was *SMART.* A-stars across the board smart. Undoubtedly the most academically gifted student I had ever encountered. But at least there was only one of him. At university, I found myself surrounded by Williams.

My academic performance significantly contributed to my self-image, so it was difficult to come to terms with what was happening. 'The first year doesn't count,' was what I repeatedly told myself in order to justify my lack of motivation and keep the cognitive dissonance at bay. I was Acutely aware of the fact that, unlike my time at secondary school and college, I didn't know anybody at the university. There were no pre-developed friendships to fall back on, so I would have to step out of my comfort zone and be more outgoing. My initial efforts of gregariousness were mildly successful. Or so I thought. It turned out that I was benefitting from other students finding their bearings during the first couple of weeks. The initial acquaintances I made faded and it felt like I had wasted the window of opportunity. Everything happened at a lightning pace. I blinked my eyes and it appeared that tight-knit social groups had already begun to crystallise. I was immediately on the outside, looking inwards. Fortunately, I was never explicitly ostracised but I spent the first year of university on the periphery of various friendship circles. I swayed like the wind seeking genuine connections. I wasn't a fan of the drinking and partying culture but I participated, nonetheless.

I prided myself on attendance and punctuality and kept the 100% attendance certificates from secondary school. But even though I lived five minutes away from the lecture theatre, I was still often late. Hundreds of students would pour into the theatre and once the large black doors were closed, you knew you were late.

I really dreaded the operations management module but still managed to drag myself out of bed. I glanced at my watch and noticed the time — whether I would make it to the hall before the door closed was fifty-fifty. The race was on. I quickened my pace, and the only thing that separated me from a speed walker was the swivel of the hips. As I entered the hallway that leads to the lecture hall, I saw a sight that sent a shiver down my spine. I wasn't fast enough. The door was closed. I placed my ear closer to the door and listened. The lecture had begun. The choice was simple, I could either walk into the theatre and have 200 faces simultaneously turn and stare at me. Or... I could go home and wait for the slides to be posted. I chose to go home.

The academic slump would continue into the second year. In conjunction to letting my standards drop educationally, I also let myself go in terms of health and fitness, finding temporary solace in fried and sugary foods.

I ate and ate, eventually ballooning up to 100+ kilograms, which for my 5"9' frame was debilitating. It was as if all semblance of self-control left me. Essentially, I was just going through the motions, doing just enough to get by, and as it turned out, no amount of calories could fill my emotional void.

My undergraduate course was four years long and included a mandatory sandwich year in year three. Ideally, students would start work placements in the summer of 2011. I was still searching in January 2012. It was a ridiculous situation. The university tried to help with motivation with an educational workshop late in the year. Getting my foot in the door was not the problem, it was the interview that was my Achilles heel.

Years of watching American sitcoms had given me a false perception of what university life would entail. Nobody told me that the universe had a strong sense of irony. How could it be that thousands of students surrounded me, but despite this, my loneliness was at an all-time high?

Time was running out and all of the billion dollar companies had already filled their quota of student work placements. I expanded my search to lesser known companies. I found a position offering a work placement in the marketing department with a salary of £23,000. It was perfect. I poured my heart and my soul into the cover letter, going through each sentence with a fine tooth comb. Once I was happy with the state of my CV, I sent off my application. The next day, I received an email inviting me to an interview. *This is surely the one,* I thought.

I practised questions and researched the company, making sure that I would impress them with my knowledge of the industry. I went to bed feeling quietly confident.

I dressed up in a blue suit and tied a laughable knot around my neck. My mode of transport was the bus and I made sure to arrive extra early so I could do some additional practice. The panel interview started off rocky but I found my stride after a few poorly answered questions. I struggled to make eye contact and couldn't decide what to do with my arms. *Should I place them on the table or below? I wonder how I am coming across. Am I smiling enough or too much?* On and on it went. By now I had grown accustomed to the monkey in my brain, bouncing around, always finding something to be anxious about.

I shook the hand of the interviewers and waited with bated breath for the phone call or email. A couple days later, a notification popped up on my email app. The subject heading indicated that it was job related.

Dear Mr Egbuonu,

Thank you for expressing interest in the marketing position and for attending the interview. Unfortunately, after careful consideration we have...

I didn't finish the email and placed my phone on the table. A few tears dropped onto my cold cheeks. After a few minutes of sitting and processing emotions, these same tears had dried up, along with all hope of finding a work placement.

I had a black notebook that I used to keep track of applications. Striking through each unsuccessful application became routine; I was used to the feeling at this point. I'm pretty sure I was one of if not *the* last person in my course to secure a work placement. I was so close to calling it quits. With a masochistic fervour, I scrolled through the LinkedIn profiles of my coursemates, who of course, had updated their information to include their work placements — Microsoft, HSBC, Barclays, BMW. Each blue-chip company I read was an arrow to my heart. *What's wrong with me? Why can't I be normal like the rest of my peers?* To add insult to injury, I would subsequently login to Facebook and Instagram and see my coursemates posting photos of them on holiday. These trips were funded with their placement money. *I should be out there with them.* I fantasised and lived vicariously through their photos for a few minutes before logging off social media altogether.

Despite the overwhelming urge to just drop out and try something else, I persisted and ended up with a work placement in the end. However, the position that I secured was unpaid, which laid the foundation for the financial woes that I would encounter early in my final year. How I stretched the five pounds per day to cover food, travel, and everything else, only God knows. Imposing austerity upon myself was the only option.

The first half of the final year was particularly bleak. Between the financial woes and being estranged from my cousin — who went to another university in Birmingham but had now left the country — I struggled. The ripple effects of the unpaid placement meant that I had to live in the cheapest accommodation possible. Here I was, a final year student living on campus with first year students. The dynamic was a bit awkward but with time, I was able to adapt. Upon meeting the first year students, I agreed to drink with them before heading out to a local nightclub. The first few drinks went down well and it was now time to head downstairs to the cab. I have no recollection of what happened next, but apparently, I overdid it and ended up in Accident & Emergency.

The nurse removed the ECG sensors that were attached to my skin and quickly ushered me out of bed. A cab arrived shortly and drove me back to the campus. What kind of first impression had I made? I couldn't tell if I had lost the respect of my peers or gained it as some hard-core binge-drinker. Getting blackout drunk on day one set the tone for the final year. My mood and general self-esteem continued to reach new lows. I even had to borrow some emergency funds from the university. With nowhere else to turn, I made the decision to undergo counselling from the university therapist. Speaking to a stranger about my struggles provided a much needed outlet for the negative thoughts that were bouncing around in my head. All in all, I received about ten sessions and was also prescribed antidepressants. I didn't have the confidence to tell anybody about my decision to see a counsellor out of fear of being stigmatised.

After a very rocky start, my financial issues were sorted out. Between that and the counselling, my confidence began to increase and each small victory added a small amount of momentum. Slowly but surely things were falling into place and my motivation was on the incline.

At this point, I had made peace with my social situation and thus felt less pressure to try and fit in. Time was running out but I remained convinced that this academic year was still salvageable. It would require a herculean effort but I was prepared to give it my best shot. After all, I had nothing to lose having already invested three years into this degree. I joined some sporting societies and also the debating club. It took a few weeks to clean up my nutrition but once I locked in a training and eating regime, the progress began to snowball. The debating society was a great fit for me and it was there that my interest in public speaking blossomed. The seeds were sown for what would go onto be my future vocation. I approached both my physical training and academics with a high intensity. My efforts would pay off as I trimmed down to a lean 78 kilos and also outperformed my own expectations academically. I could hardly believe that I achieved first class honours after a disastrous three years. This degree was surely a reward from God for surviving such an arduous four years.

CHAPTER TWO

TRANSFIGURATION

G raduation is usually a day of celebration and festivity; unfortunately, that wasn't the case for me. It was a day that I quietly dreaded. Of course, I took a sense of pride from my academic achievements. After all, this is an aspect that had largely shaped my self-image up to this point. The single-mindedness that I had on the road to university had ran out of steam now that I had reached my destination. I wasn't sure about what I wanted to do with my life. In a sense, my enrolment had bought me a precious four years to figure things out. The West Midlands had served me well but going back to London was one of the few things that was guaranteed.

The weather was pleasant in Birmingham, with spring in full effect. The temperature was in the mid-20s and a mild breeze sliced through the air. Inside the auditorium were hundreds of students draped in different combinations of ceremonial gowns.

Sir Ken Robinson delivered an excellent speech. I became aware of him through his 2006 TED talk, "Do Schools Kill Creativity?"

"Every one of us creates our own life... To be a human being is a creative act," resonated with me.

Eager to avoid embarrassment, I carefully studied the movements of the students as they walked up a small flight of stairs to collect their diplomas. I pictured myself stumbling up the steps or botching the handshake. Why my mind chose to torment me with these imagined scenarios, I would never know. Surely, this level of neuroticism wasn't normal. Maybe, life would be more enjoyable if I was less cerebral and focused more energy on the external world. I often felt powerless to stop the constant waves of negative and anxious thoughts.

My brother and mother watched as I collected the diploma from the university chancellor. I successfully navigated the steps, shook his hands, and flashed an awkward smile. Following that, I swiftly marched back down the steps, eager to join my loved ones.

It was a beautiful moment, but the positive feelings were short-lived as I was perilously close to confronting the question of what comes next. Despite the embarrassing state of my finances, I managed to cobble together enough money for a decent framed photo.

The happiness from the graduation ceremony quickly wore off and it became apparent that I had no idea what I wanted to do with my career. The protective bubble of the university had burst. No more deferring career choices until I graduated.

Once I returned to London, there wasn't any time to rest on my laurels. My student loan was quickly drying up and the company that I did my "work placement" with didn't have the resources to take me on as a paid employee. It was back to the dreaded job hunt. Internet tabs from the biggest recruitment websites were strewn across my browser.

The year was 2013 and the economy was showing some signs of recovery following the 2007 financial crisis. I probably would have struggled to find a job, regardless of the economic situation.

The job application process was exhausting and conveying enthusiasm through cover letters became increasingly difficult. I was convinced the corporate world was where I was destined to be — where I could glance at the London skyline from the window of a massive skyscraper. The rapid job rejections soon brought me tumbling back down to reality.

As the days passed, the roles that I considered grew more extensive to the point where I was applying almost indiscriminately to anything I was remotely qualified for.

Frustratingly, there seemed to be a never ending stream of recruitment consultant jobs, no matter where I searched. The base salaries weren't very attractive but the uncapped earning potential was certainly a draw. Unfortunately, I couldn't relate to much of the person specification as they were looking for "money-motivated, confident, and incredibly driven applicants." These qualities were strikingly absent from my personality profile.

I couldn't fathom working in a high pressure sales environment.

Seeking a break from the drudgery of job applications, I bought a ticket to Loughborough to go and visit Gabriel. It was a beautiful weekend in which all of my anxieties temporarily ceased. We smoked some cannabis and howled with laughter as we watched Ren & Stumpy videos. With each puff, my anxieties would evaporate. I put on *My Dark Twisted Fantasy* by Kanye West, secured the headphones on, and closed my eyes as I laid peacefully on the bed, taking pleasure in the discovery of small musical details that I wasn't aware of in a sober state. As the weekend drew to a close, I realised that if I had chosen Loughborough instead of Aston, I would have spent three years of university with my best friend. A deep sense of regret washed over me.

Was history about to repeat itself? It felt like the second year of university all over again. I persisted with the applications and I eventually secured a sales role. The job was definitely not located in Canary Wharf or Liverpool Street and I had no briefcase. Cold calling was extremely uncomfortable and I never fully acclimated with the fact that my colleagues could listen to my conversations. Despite this, I soldiered on as the trajectory of the company sloped downwards. Employees were leaving the *Titanic* and by the start of 2015, I was unemployed.

I tried a different approach this time and was focused more on quality over quantity. By random chance, I stumbled across a job title with the heading: "Young Black Men's Project Officer." It piqued my interest, and the more I read about the role, the more excited I became.

As I read through the job description, I mentally cross-referenced my experiences with the job specifications. This was the closest thing to a dream job that I had seen. I tempered my excitement and meticulously put an application together. The interview went reasonably well and I did not have to put on a façade for the interviewers.

It was back day at the gym and I was in full flow when an unexpected call paused my workout. To my surprise, I had been offered the position. I would soon be working to inspire young black boys in the borough of Hackney, a cause that was very close to my heart. Things were beginning to fall into place.

Permanent teeth begin erupting at age 6, and continue until age 21. Here I was aged 25 but I still had two of my baby teeth; a perfect symbol of my stunted growth. The teeth were so loose that the best option was to get them removed. I didn't have enough money for implants so dentures were the next best thing. My mind had plenty of things to worry about and now being seen without my dentures was quickly racing up the list of fears.

The role was everything I hoped it would be. Finally, I was making a difference. The job involved a great deal of human interaction. I was liaising with council executives, business professionals, and cohorts of young people who had signed up for the programme. The project was energising and I was acutely aware of the responsibilities that I had. The feeling of inadequacy raged. My introverted and reserved demeanour would surely prevent me from achieving maximal success in the role. As the face of the project, I had to coordinate the different strands and be present during board meetings. One particular session involved high-level executives from the council and the CEO of the charity I worked for. As the meeting drew on, I found myself wanting to contribute, but the anxiety robbed me of my voice. After introducing myself,

I did not utter a single word. This disappointment was palpable. How could I be the face of the project if I couldn't speak with conviction? I needed a remedy. The details of my anxiety were subsequently shared with my GP. Due to my history with poor mental health at university, a new prescription of Citalopram, an antidepressant, was made available. I hoped the medication would be the silver bullet that would enable me to conquer my fears and put a dampener on the negative thoughts.

Another chemical was introduced to my treatment cocktail. This one, however, was illicit. Like oil and water, the two substances should not have been mixed, but I didn't care for or appreciate the risks. Live and let live. The cannabis provided relief from anxious thoughts and was a much-needed reprieve. My history with the substance is an unconventional one. I was not introduced to weed via peer pressure. The choice to seek it out came from what I deemed a rational solution to the predicament I faced. My first usage was after a stressful period at university, but I did not experiment with it much after that. However, in 2015, the smoking habit was picked up again. This intermingling of cannabis and Citalopram did not cross my mind as something that could be problematic, and for weeks, this was the cocktail of illicit and licit substances I undertook. The usage increased, and it became less of a recreational tool and more of a crutch. The simultaneous mixing of the anti-depressants soon stopped and cannabis became my chief medication.

What followed was an almost seamless change in my fortunes. I noticed that I was suddenly more outspoken and forceful when it came to the meetings and just speaking my mind in general. I relished this feeling. The formula was producing results, so naturally, I doubled down and continued to do what was working for me. I was navigating social situations with a newfound swagger and confidence. Even though I studied business, my interest had never been this pronounced and I was inundated with business ideas and opportunities.

So this is what it feels like to be on the other side of fear. Through no action of my own, I no longer cared about what people thought of me. This is true freedom.

Bill Gates and Mark Zuckerberg were no longer rare success stories but would soon be looked at as competition. Emotions seemed more visceral and for the first time in my life, I was alive. I felt connected with nature and the universe as a whole. The beauty of the clouds had never been more apparent. Thus, I dedicated thousands of megabytes to candid outdoor photography. This connection to the universe was wholly apparent and it seemed to guide my actions. So-called "random events" had a purpose and life was a big game, a game in which I had just received the cheat code. Ideas were in the ether and I would just retrieve them with consummate ease. With the new ideas and confidence also came an abundance of energy.

Life was fantastic. I was sleeping less but feeling more energised. My 6 a.m. risings turned into 5 a.m. risings and before I knew it, I was operating effectively with under two hours of sleep. This seemed counterintuitive, as surely, having less sleep should have reduced my energy levels and overall physical wellbeing. Still, in my case, it was proving to be beneficial. Unable to accurately grasp what was happening, I was keen to maximise these newfound *abilities*. With this energy also came a greater sense of curiosity. Life seemed more exciting and my every emotion — whether anger or joy — was amplified.

For the first time in a long time, things were beginning to fall into place. Presentations were delivered with more conviction and my self-esteem was skyrocketing. With nuclear force, the shell that had constrained was blown to bits. Freedom. I now stood triumphantly on the other side of fear. A place where doubt no longer existed.

My productivity level increased exponentially and I jumped out of bed with a determination to seize the day. Ideas, like pinballs, continued to course through my mind. Before I could fully engage with one thought, another idea had captured my attention. Billions of neurons were simultaneously firing, pushing me into a state of constant creativity. I was galvanised and determined to pursue the ideas and manifest them into reality. My biggest problem was not having enough time to execute these ideas and plans. I had a little notebook where I would jot them down. I misplaced my notebook but wasn't worried in the slightest because I had direct access and could download ideas from the most creative force in the universe, God.

What was happening to me? I had no idea, but I fully embraced it. It was as if I had unlocked this whole new level of human potential. Conversations were fluid, the words just rolling off my tongue. On a typical day, I tended to speak in tangents, but in this new state of mind, I weaved between topics with Muhammad Ali-like precision. I didn't care whether the poor soul on the other end could keep up. Often, my conversation partners were too polite to end the conversation. On one occasion, my feature-length rant only ended after the intervention of a third party.

When I first watched *The Matrix* in 1999, I was blown away by the storytelling and the special effects. It quickly became an all-time favourite. I pulled the blu ray and popped it inside my PC. This time was different. I received a message from the movie. The esoteric meaning of the movie was crystal clear. The film was speaking directly to me: YOU ARE THE ONE. Empowered by this newfound information, I made it my mission to help people. For years, my circle of compassion was very small and only included myself. However, now the circle of compassion encompasses the earth. I didn't see anything that distinguished me from anybody. Underneath the skin, we share the same divine essence.

My relationship with money could've been better. Saving wasn't something I had prioritised and I was drowning in my student overdraft. With that being said, my credit was decent and I had built up some good habits in that area. I was given a credit card as a perk for opening a student bank account, though the limit was quite low.

With only that meagre prompting, down the YouTube rabbit hole I went. I spent a gob-smacking amount of time watching videos of the history of money and how we went from currency backed by gold to fiat currency. The game was rigged and I would beat it with my credit scheme.

I had it all figured out. I would apply for a credit card and use one to pay off the other. It was a fool-proof plan, and my job would support me through this process. I would max out my credit and then declare bankruptcy.

It was in Dalston Supermarket where I signed up for the first credit card. Those salespeople I usually tactically avoid made a compelling case. Once the first credit card arrived, I wanted to see how far I could take this.

Like a child on Christmas morning, I struggled to contain my excitement as I waited for my cards to arrive. The routine of the postman was identified, and I waited with bated breath until I heard that sound of cascading letters. The postman was Santa Claus and each envelope he delivered was analysed enthusiastically. There was a feeling of bliss when I felt the plastic card with my name embedded.

Next were the payday loans, with each lender more than happy to lend me money at extortionate interest rates.

I bought a new laptop; it was mid-range, but a badly needed upgrade from my old one which was on its last legs. Not a week had passed when I came to the realisation that my editing needs would require a more powerful laptop. At this point, I had created the "Matrix in Life" podcast and had plans to venture into video content. A future-proof notebook would be a wise investment, so I entered the URL for a PC and laptop customising website, opting for a 32GB ram, 1TB hard drive, the latest i7 processor, second battery, printer, etc. In short, I selected the best option for each category. The total was over £2000.

Shopping had never provided this much of a thrill. For whatever reason, it was now one of the most pleasing activities I could engage in. My credit card would fund Uber trips to all manner of shops. I also purchased copious amounts of cannabis. The most ridiculous purchase I made was a vinyl record player. I didn't know the unit required assembly. This was the most challenging assembly process I had encountered. Ultimately, I admitted my defeat and eventually returned the record player.

This was impulsive retail therapy. I was a child with no filter and deep pockets and there were sweet shops on every street corner. Another new investment was a £200 hat, 566% more than what I usually spend on a hat.

One time, in Boots, I spent over £90 on male grooming products. I also thought that with all these business ventures, I would need to buy another phone line, and I did just that. I maxed out all the credit cards within a week of receiving them. I also began to give generously to homeless people. I realised that it was they who needed my help the most. I saw myself as a superhero and my power was credit.

There was one gentleman I met during my adventures who bore the hallmarks of a rough sleeper. I did not have the money on me at that precise moment, so I gave him my number and told him where to meet me the next day. I was a crusader, fighting homelessness on the mean streets of London, one ATM withdrawal at a time.

Spending money was one of the few things that were more exciting than receiving cash. I travelled in Ubers like the young budding CEO I was. No distance was too short and no expense would be spared. Dalston was my spiritual home and it was where I spent a great deal of my money. While traipsing along the high street, I noticed a vendor who bought and sold goods and entered his shop. The colour scheme was red and yellow and electrical devices decorated the glass cabinet on each side of the entrance. I unloaded a laptop, which had only been purchased the week prior. The shop assistant inspected the item and plugged some details into his computer. He subsequently revealed the price he was willing to pay. I was horrified by the quote and decided to take my business elsewhere. I wheeled my little suitcase down the high street and back to my home. I had too much energy for a bus ride.

It was only once I had settled down that I realised I was missing something. The laptop. The last place I remember having it was the buyer and seller in Dalston. I wasn't 100% certain, though. It was evening and the shop was probably closed. It was around noon the next day when I made the return journey. The shop assistant flashed a bewildered expression when I explained the situation.

The shopkeeper squared up to me. *How unprofessional of you*, I thought. *Resorting to threats of physical violence.* However, my thoughts and speech were not in sync. I began goading him on. The sense of danger was almost seductive.

It's almost as if I felt this compulsion to speak. Despite the shopkeeper's apparent confusion, I continued to plead my case and I was now making it clear that the police would be involved if necessary. Perhaps I could have delivered the message without being so snarky and sarcastic.

It was then I realised that my new gift of gab could get me into trouble. The shopkeeper aggressively drove towards me while shouting and proclaiming his innocence. I pointed out that any acts of violence would be picked up by the CCTV cameras sprinkled across the shop. Perhaps it was the realisation that there were witnesses around that made the shopkeeper change his tone or maybe he experienced a grand epiphany. He ventured into the backroom and rummaged through some boxes.

After what seemed like an eternity, he emerged with the same laptop that, five minutes prior, he had no recollection of ever coming into contact with.

I could not stay away from Dalston during the summer of 2015. I was excited to be amid fellow business people who had control of their destinies. I dragged my mini-suitcase around with me everywhere. Once again, I found myself in the Kingsland shopping centre. Before I headed into the computer exchange shop, an Eastern European gentleman approached me. He flashed the latest Samsung smartphone, asking, 'Want to buy this phone? I'll make you a good deal.'

It must be my lucky day, I thought. So I followed the man outside of the store to his car, which he'd parked around the corner. He seemed to be in a rush and moved with urgency.

There was another man inside the vehicle, and they asked me to get in. Once inside, he gave me the phone to examine, and while I was doing that, he also brought out a laptop and a tablet. He said he would do a deal for me. However, he wanted to know how much money I had available. His demeanour was a mixture of panicky and pushy. If I said one thing that he didn't like, he seemed ready to call everything off in an instant. I told them that I didn't have any cash on me, but I would check my newly received credit card. He followed me to the cashpoint.

I was so eager that I left my suitcase outside of his car as I went to the ATM. I withdrew everything I could from that card. We went back into the car, and the transaction was complete. He handed me a little black suitcase which contained both the phone and the tablet. Something was exciting about buying apparently stolen goods. He counted the money and then threw it onto the dashboard. *Pleasure doing business with you*, I thought as I left the vehicle, but before I could thank them, the door slammed shut, and the car zoomed into the distance. It all happened in a flash. I grabbed my suitcase and headed home, excited to see the fruits of this transaction.

Once inside, I opened the black case, only to find newspapers inside. It was all a big con. I grew up watching the real hustle, and the mantra was simple, "If it's too good to be true, it probably is." I congratulated them for their cleverness and quickly shook off the whole ordeal.

My interactions at work changed, mostly for the better. I was able to articulate myself with more confidence and I no longer was afraid to let my opinion be known. These changes were appraised as positive initially by both family members and work colleagues.

It didn't last long, though. I grew increasingly suspicious about the motives of my superiors at work. They were trying to stifle my vision. A call was made about me behind my back and once I became aware of this, my frustration reached the point of no return. It was then that I knew that my fate was inevitable.

It was a beautiful summer morning, a day destined for productivity. I strolled into the office with my small, golden luggage bag, greeting the secretary as I made my way through the reception. In a relaxed tone of voice, I uttered the words, 'I quit.' I explained the lack of support that I felt, confident in the belief that I could do a better job on my own. My co-worker and my manager pulled their jaws from the floor and attempted to reason with me. I wasn't having any of it. They mentioned the fact that I couldn't suddenly quit. I pulled out the contract and reminded them that I was still within the probation period. I grabbed my suitcase and headed out. The secretary, who exuded warmth and care, tried to make me reconsider my position, but I politely declined and left the building.

This summer, I had become aware of the existence of the international slavery museum in Liverpool. Visiting it would surely benefit the young people who were part of the Young Black Men's Project at work. I felt like I was not being supported in this decision and so, the seeds that would lead to me inexplicably resigning were sown. After quitting my job, I decided that it would be worthwhile visiting the museum on my own. I timed my visit so that it coincided with international slavery remembrance day on August 23rd. The exhibit was wide-ranging, featuring comprehensive artefacts and information about transatlantic and modern slavery. Sometime during my stay, I lost my wallet, and I tried not to let it dampen my spirits. I didn't know why I was suddenly so forgetful. This became a recurring theme throughout the summer.

Following the powerful experience at the museum, I decided that I needed to start a summer school. Even though I wasn't employed by the charity anymore, I would start my own Young Black Men's Project. I secured the keys to a local youth club and recruited a handful of teenagers. I invited some elders from the community and we discussed history, society, and everything in between in a productive generational dialogue.

So, I found myself once again in Dalston, East London at the Kingsland shopping centre. My trusty suitcase was in hand and contained a variety of wares, from electronics to random books. I posted up in the middle of the centre, carefully selecting the location that would cause the most chaos.

The owner of the popcorn stall to the left of me was up in arms as I was violating his prime location. I ignored his pleas and carefully unzipped the suitcase, revealing the contents to curious passers-by. Once I was happy with my set-up, the auction began. I channelled my inner Sunday market trader and triumphantly announced that all items must go.

Slowly but steadily, a crowd began to emerge in a dome-like manner as people's curiosity began to grow. It wasn't a great auction to be fair, as I was giving things away for free randomly. The laptop was one of the first things to be given away.

At first, the people in attendance were apprehensive about taking the items from me. Still, once they saw that I meant business, it became natural to them. The security guard stood posted to the left of me, radio in hand. He wasn't sure what to make of the situation, so he radioed his superior. I told the crowd that he was trying to end the giveaway, and he quickly felt the wrath of the people. When his superiors asked him what offence I had committed, he struggled to get his response out. Something along the lines of, 'He is in the middle of the market...giving away his belongings?' I couldn't help but laugh at their correspondence, but I wouldn't let that stop me. *People donate things to charity shops every day. What's the big deal?* I thought. *I'm doing the same thing, but I'm cutting out the middleman.*

Next to go was the smartwatch. I removed it from my left hand and asked the crowd, 'Who wants this watch?' The stench of consumerism radiated from the mob; the people couldn't believe their luck. My prerequisite to giving these items away was simple. I would ask the people, 'Am I crazy?' over and over again. If they said no, then I would hand them the goods. With the smartwatch, the lucky recipient was a teenager of South American descent. He was there with his friend. He took the watch somewhat reluctantly and headed off. A few minutes later, the boy returned the watch to me, saying that he couldn't accept it.

I was shocked by this as nobody else even hesitated to take the items from me, let alone return them. His conscience must have been working overtime. There was some faith in society, after all. The feeling of hope dissipated quickly. A lady who had already collected a couple of items wasted no time in stating that if he didn't want it, she would be happy to take it off my hands. I agreed and passed it over. Apparently, she needed it more than me. It was interesting that the assortment of books that were in the suitcase received little attention compared to the electrical gizmos. Once the electronics had dried up, I packed up shop, closed my bag, and left the shopping centre.

Letting go was a recurring theme, and I felt compelled to simplify my life. I underwent an extensive process of spring cleaning, giving my little brother the option to choose any of my clothes. Anything that he didn't pick went to charity. My sisters joined this movement, and between us, we filled 15 black bags. The fact that I had accumulated and was clinging to so much stuff disgusted and irritated me in equal measure. My enthusiasm was infectious and spread beyond the family, which led to Gabriel undergoing a mini-clear-out too.

Chapter Three
SECTION 136

The concern about my behaviour by my friends and family was frustrating. The more they pushed, the more erratic my actions became. *You want to see crazy? I can do crazy.* Finally, I was coming out of my shell and everyone was saying there was something wrong with me. They told me that I was displaying symptoms of bipolar disorder. When I heard the symptoms read aloud, I said, "It sounds like you are describing a superhero." Reduced need for sleep, heightened senses, increased confidence, happy, euphoric, energised, and creative. Who wouldn't want to be feeling this? I was NEO in *The Matrix* and the agents were trying to constrain my mind and keep me in the programme. Nobody could understand what I was going through. What I wanted the most was the freedom to pursue my interests. My threshold for all things illogical significantly reduced. One of the tactics that I employed was radio silence, giving whoever violated my sense of logic the silent treatment. The compulsion to speak was, at times, overwhelming, and it took some effort to control my impulses.

I negotiated with my family members to get myself voluntarily checked out. I visited two medical institutions with one of my oldest friends. We weren't aware of the protocol. It wasn't like physical ailments where the procedures are clear and so we visited the nearest facilities with the NHS logo emblazoned on the signage.

I was told that I could not just walk in and that I had to get referred. I explained that my parents were concerned with my mental health, and they repeated their policy. I had to make an appointment with the GP to get a referral, which could take weeks. It only takes a moment to end one's life — not that I was suicidal at that point or anything. I felt vindicated by this, I had done my part, demonstrating my ability to compromise.

My cognition was intact, but my temperament was much more volatile. When I was happy, I was euphoric, but when somebody crossed me, the rage inside me had to express itself somehow. I would maybe jump up and down or walk around the room in agitation.

I remember one argument among my family where I spoke about how worthless the qualifications that I had gained were. The dispute culminated with me ripping up my university diploma. I placed no value on western education and they could not comprehend what was happening. Remnants of the printer that I had only recently purchased laid strewn across the carpet, the result of a previous fit of rage.

Tensions continued to flare up in the household and this culminated with the abrupt decision to sleep in a hotel and collect my thoughts. Unfortunately, it was around 2:00 a.m., and I didn't understand the trouble that was to come. I gathered way too many belongings, record player included, which made the journey to the first hotel all the more exhausting. Once I got there, they told me that there were no beds available.

Fair enough, I thought, *let me try the other hotel that is local to me*. I began to regret taking all of these belongings, but my pride wouldn't let me go back and drop some items back after storming out. Going back to the family home would be admitting defeat. I needed to persevere.

Luckily, we live in the age of the app and I was able to book a cab to the hotel. Once I got there, it was the same story, no rooms available. At this point, I was beginning to question my decision, but I was determined to find a hotel. Once again, I found myself on my phone application, browsing hotels that currently have rooms available. All I wanted to do was kick back, unwind, and watch *The Matrix*. Was that asking too much? My hotel quest led me to West London at a relatively modern hotel. I thanked the cab driver as he helped me unload my belongings. Immediately, I was hit with good and bad news by the receptionist. He confirmed that they had rooms available. However, check-in was at midnight. That was no good, and so once again, I was on my phone, exhausted, searching for a hotel. Fool me once, shame on you. To be fooled thrice was surely shame on me.

This time, I would do things differently to prevent this situation from happening again. I booked a hotel room in West London and made sure that the check-in time corresponded with the time on my watch. I used the scrolling interface on my phone to select 5:00 am. I received the confirmation email which specified the check-in time. At this point, I was sure that nothing else would go wrong and it would be smooth sailing from here on out.

I arrived at the fourth hotel and told the receptionist of my booking. To my dismay, he repeated the same thing that I heard at the last hotel. Check-in is at 12:00 am. I asked the man if I could at least stay in the lobby, and he told me no.

At this point, I had reached my limit and decided rather spontaneously that I was going to wait right there in the lobby until it was time to check-in. You can call it my version of a peaceful protest. What I couldn't understand was why you would allow me to choose my check-in time via the app only to be told otherwise in person. A whole bunch of hassle would not have occurred.

And so, the war of attrition began, customers of the hotel walked around me because my belongings occupied the reception. I could see how this was impacting the manager and he grew increasingly uncomfortable. I was very relaxed, biding my time, and ignoring the pleas to leave as I'd been misled by the application. About half an hour into the standoff, the manager said he would call the police if I didn't leave. I encouraged him to do so as I had a right to be here. Within 10 minutes, two police officers arrived at the scene. The manager explained from his perspective what the situation was, and I was going about my own business, initially giving the police radio silence. I was curious to see how much taxpayer money would be wasted in dealing with this situation.

Eventually, I broke my vow of silence and began conversing with the officer. I explained what I was doing there and made clear my intentions to stay until I could check into my room. For a good 45 minutes, the policeman tried his hardest to get me to reconsider my decision, but I was adamant. I did, however, extend an olive branch to the manager and told him that if he apologised for the misleading hotel booking application, I would leave. However, the pride of the manager overwhelmed him. He refused to apologise. Instead, his employee gave me what I considered to be a sincere apology. This was not sufficient as he had done no wrong to me. The manager's stance was firm. He wasn't going to apologise, and I wasn't going to leave. At this point, the officer called backup, and within moments, there were about four police officers in the hotel reception.

I joked with the officer that he was "messing with a billionaire." It was a silly reference to the hyperinflation in Zimbabwe, where one dollar was equivalent to 35 trillion Zimbabwean dollars, but the officer could not read my mind and clearly wasn't amused.

The stalemate continued until around 7:00 a.m. when the manager told the officers and me that he had officially cancelled my booking and that I now had no right to be there. Soon, the police officers established their authority over me. One mentioned the breach of peace laws would allow him to remove me from the premises. I said, 'Do what you have to do, officer.' Before I knew it, the cold steel of the handcuffs encircled my wrists. It was my first time under arrest, and my immediate thought was that the cuffs were way too tight.

The officer then escorted me downstairs and carried my belongings down also. I thought this whole exercise was just for show, and that once I was outside of the building, we would part ways. We had now left the private property and the officer stated that he was un-arresting me from the breach of peace. However, he was now detaining me under Section 136 of the Mental Health Act.

First, I was in awe; then I had to give the officer some respect for this sneaky manoeuvre. He could have made his intentions clear in the hotel lobby, but Section 136 is only applicable to public property. My right to liberty vanished by this simple application of the law. Looking back at things, I have to commend the officer as he executed a perfect combo of legislation smoothly, from breach of peace to Section 136.

Section 136 enables the police officer(s) to take an individual who they deem to be suffering from a mental disorder and to be in immediate need of care or control to a "place of safety." They do this in the interests of that individual or for the protection of others. The two places of safety are a hospital and a police station. You can be held for up to 72 hours while an approved mental health professional with specialist training assesses you.

This whole saga was surreal and it certainly wasn't as straightforward as it could have been. At one point, I was in the police van waiting for what seemed to be an eternity to go to the hospital. I repeatedly asked for my cuffs to be loosened but my pleas fell on deaf ears. There was a young officer in the van and I asked him, 'Why are you treating me like a criminal? Can you at least loosen these handcuffs? I am in pain.' I tried to catch his eyes but he could not bring himself to look at me squarely.

Eventually, the officer hopped in the van and we were off to the hospital. It was a slightly bumpy ride with no real care for my well-being. *How come they have seatbelts and I am swaying side to side, bumping into the walls of the vehicle, with my hands cuffed behind my back?* After 15 minutes or so, we reached our destination and the officers and medical professionals spoke among themselves. I was un-cuffed and asked to sit down in this hospital in West London.

The approved mental health professional from the NHS spoke with the officers who I dealt with at the hotel and gave their version of the whole ordeal. The police stayed at the hospital for about half an hour. They did this probably to make sure I wasn't a physical threat or something. Shortly after that, they departed and I began speaking with the NHS woman. From the outset, she suggested that I needed to be sectioned and taken to the ward. For the first time during this whole episode, I began to fear that I would lose my freedom. I tried my best to explain my actions and the situation at home that led to this. Even the jokes I made with the officers became proof of mental illness. Note to self: Do not joke with the police. What you say can and will be used against you in the court of mental health assessment.

What was interesting was the fact that in the room were two independent mental health consultants. They sat to my right while the NHS professional sat on my left, rapidly typing away at her computer. I don't know what she was typing at the time, but she could have at least addressed me face to face. At this point, I thought it was a foregone conclusion that I would enter the mental health system, and she was preparing the paperwork right there and then. What happened afterwards filled me with both relief and astonishment.

The NHS woman was adamant that there was something wrong with me. However, independent consultants had the power to overrule her verdict. They deemed me sane enough to go home, sleep it off, and make amends with my family. They listened carefully to my reasoning and they could see that my logic and cognition was indeed intact. The different judgements shocked me as it revealed the subjective nature of psychiatry as a medical practice. One professional said I was mentally ill and should be placed under a section, and on the other front, I was being told to go home. How could three specialists come to different conclusions? I was relieved that I wouldn't be hospitalised, but the lack of consistency in their determination was telling.

It seems beliefs and biases can impact the conclusions that medical professionals arrive at following the assessment. No brain scans were taken or any physical tests that could substantiate her claims. It was her opinion and her observations against mine.

Once discharged, I was glad to be on my way home. Regardless of the drama occurring domestically, I would rather be in a familiar environment with my freedom than to enter the mental health system. I was picked up by my friends and family who I was delighted to see. They loaded up all my belongings in the car in a Tetris-like manner, not to mention the four passengers. I recall carrying electronics on my lap for the duration of the ride home. This whole episode occurred on September 5.

CHAPTER FOUR

FAMILY TENSION

A few days had passed since the Section 136 episode. Tensions in the household began to rise again. Things culminated in a confrontation with friends and family which led to me breaking my golden rule: "Do not lose control of your emotions." It was a cross between a chess match and a video game and my big brother was the final boss. Thinking a few steps ahead was essential.

At one point, family and friends gathered round to stage an intervention. It was frustrating because I was missing out on crucial business opportunities. However, I knew I had an ace up my sleeve. Unlike most of humanity, I was able to function without sleep and I knew if I was patient enough, eventually, everybody would doze off. Minutes turned into hours. I kept my thoughts bottled up. This was a war of attrition and my victory was assured. As the clock passed midnight, I glanced up from the chair and noticed that everybody was finally asleep. It was time to paint the town red.

I carried my passport with me in a Nike side bag, ready to leave the country at a moment's notice. In all honesty, if the police did not detain me under Section 136, I would've travelled to Amsterdam. As a form of damage limitation, a situation emerged where I wasn't permitted to leave the house. A prisoner in my own home, this was unacceptable. The walls felt like they were closing in on me as my anxiety continued to ramp up. I had to escape. I had traded in my phone, and I was yet to purchase a new one with the store credit. I needed to access a telephone and call the police, as I could count on them to end my captivity. I moved around the house scheming and plotting.

The landline in the living room was my golden ticket. Playing the long game was essential. Be inconspicuous, I told myself, and disguise your intentions. Patience is indeed a virtue, and my perseverance paid off as I took advantage of an opening, retrieving the landline and dialling 999. Being a police officer in London must throw up a myriad of strange scenarios. This was definitely one of those occasions. The officers arrived after 10 minutes or so. The moment the officers knocked on the door, I knew the battle was over. Checkmate. I explained the situation to them, emphasising my prisoner status, before stepping out of the house and embracing the fresh air in my lungs. Upon leaving the house, I just strolled around the neighbourhood. The most important thing was that I was no longer caged within those four walls. It was evening time, and every shop was closed, so after a couple of hours, I went home and failed to get a good night's sleep.

I was making the most of my new top-of-the-range laptop. Applications would instantly open and there was enough RAM for me to run as many programs as I saw fit. On my YouTube travails, I had encountered a host of conspiracy theories. Things finally began to make sense as I saw the world for what it was. I stepped into the kitchen to whip up a coffee, and when I returned, I gazed fixedly at my laptop screen. What I saw perplexed me. My mouse cursor was moving frantically across the screen as if it had a mind of its own. *They're watching me*, I thought. *Who else can be behind this but the government? They want me to believe that I am crazy, and this serves as an exercise of their powers.*

I finally knew where GCHQ was spending its research and development funds. I closed the screen and tried to gather my thoughts. As I paced around the room, I struggled to think of an appropriate response. Was any form of communication safe? My WhatsApp conversations? Surely, my phone lines were being tapped at this point. *The government must be in cahoots with my family members, and they are orchestrating things to impede my progress and prevent me from fulfilling my goals. I could not let them stop me.*

The next day, I went to Argos and purchased a Logitech mouse in the hopes that this would prevent the government from remotely controlling my computer. Some family members had arrived, and I went to the living room to greet them. After exchanging formalities, I ventured back into my room. To my dismay, the cyberattacks had increased, not only was my mouse cursor shaking violently, but the orientation of my screen had rotated

180 degrees. Many chills rippled down my spine. The laptop was only a few weeks old, and in my 25 years on the planet, I had never encountered anything like this. I consider myself reasonably adept at computing, but I could not make heads or tails of this. Therefore, my assumption that this was from the government was the only rational conclusion available.

I had implemented a rule which stated that nobody should be in my room so I could get some peace. I was under house arrest and even when I managed to leave the flat, family members were following me. I was not allowed to purchase anything once they told the shopkeeper that I was mentally unwell. They had good intentions, but I just wanted to be left alone to figure things out.

My friends and family broke my new rule and entered my room uninvited. What followed was a showdown and confrontation. During the back and forth, in an adrenaline-filled moment, I struck the radiator with my left hand with enough force to damage the pipes. Water was pouring onto the carpet and, at that point, my friends and family had seen enough. They held me down and sought police intervention. It was not the first time I had dealt with the police, mind you. On the other occasions, they turned up with an ambulance but I let them know about the human rights act and my right to liberty. I knew that as long as I did not try and harm myself or others that they could not take me in. They knew that I was clued up and they were powerless. This radiator incident was indeed the tipping point, the straw that broke the camel's back.

My friends subdued me until the police arrived. I tried my best to shake them off, wriggling violently and screaming at the top of my lungs as if I were possessed. But my efforts were in vain and after exhausting my energy, I yielded. It was a surreal experience. The people who had held me down emotionally and socially were now literally holding me down. The police shortly arrived at the house, navigating the various obstacles to get to me.

It was probably the worst time that this could have happened, as I was planning on buying a new phone the next day. They detained me under Section 2 of the Mental Health Act with no access to the outside world. I went into custody without resistance as they placed the handcuffs on my wrists for the second time in the summer.

I sat adjacent to the police officers, in what seemed to be an everlasting ride. I couldn't help but relive the radiator incident. The sound of traffic penetrated the deafening silence in the police van. I had no idea what the next steps would be. As we reached the destination, a mixture of curiosity and anxiety enveloped me.

I was escorted out of the van and into a building with a cold and empty aura. *This is a strange mental hospital,* I thought, not that I had anything to compare it to.

My belt and shoelaces were collected by one of the officials. Upon giving my details to the police, one officer told me that I would get a room and a bed. "Ensuite" was the particular term that he used. In a swift motion, I was ushered into a room and the door slammed shut. As I gazed outwards, the gravity of the situation became apparent.

My worst fear had come to pass; I had lost my freedom. I looked at the rice and sweet chilli ready meal in disgust. Eating was the last thing I wanted to do. For the life of me, I couldn't understand why I was in this place. Maybe I had watched too much American TV, as I was expecting some bars or something. The room resembled a vault — just me, the blue mat, blue pillow, toilet, and the intercom system. I guess this was their "place of safety." On the bed laid a faded piece of paper with the Metropolitan police logo barely visible. It contained a list of my rights while under detention. According to the law, a police station should be the last resort, after other possibilities have been exhausted.

In this case, it seemed to be the very first option. The first right on that faded piece of paper was the right to a solicitor. I pressed the intercom and asked for one. The voice on the other side told me, "We tried to call him, and he was not available." Whoever was working this intercom must think that I am a fool. I didn't even mention which solicitor I was requesting. As I continued to press the issue, the intercom operator showed his disdain for the legal process. He would cut the intercom off for about five minutes at a time because I had the nerve to request a solicitor.

I grew increasingly frustrated as time went on. I had no means of measuring time and I couldn't understand why the police had placed me in here. If, according to the officers, I am mentally unwell, then surely the last place to put me would be in an enclosed space such as this? If one breaks their arm or leg, they would expect to be taken to a hospital for treatment. The last thing that I needed in this state of mind was this purgatory-like prison experience. I'm not a convicted criminal, so why on earth was I being treated like one? The sporadic intercom disabling only made things worse. I kept asking the intercom, "How long till the police get here?" but they were not sure when they would arrive.

I was taken out of the cell twice for assessments by doctors. The way they placed me back in the cell was startling. I was handcuffed and escorted by five or six police officers into the cell. One of them shouted "face forward" as I tried to sneak a glance. Pressure was placed on my body, even though I was not resisting. It was almost as if they were trying to get me to respond aggressively. They put me on the floor and undid the handcuffs, continually reminding me to face forward. At the time, I could not understand why this whole process was necessary. They were treating me like a violent, maniacal criminal. I displayed not one iota of aggression towards the police, so when they use the term reasonable force, one had to question the necessity of this. In a smooth motion, the officer undid the handcuffs, and while I was facing forward, all five of the officers quickly scampered out of the cell and slammed the door shut. They repeated this same process verbatim the second time they placed me back in the cell.

The time I spent in the cell was soul-destroying; I felt my mind deteriorate as time went on. I wasn't interested in eating the food offered to me and I remember flushing it down the toilet. My pleas were falling on deaf ears and in that same childlike manner, the rage took over. If they were going to keep ignoring me, then I was going to create noise and havoc, so they had to listen to me.

I started by slamming the blue sleeping mat on the ground to make some noise and get their attention. This was creative destruction at its finest. I looked at my surroundings and thought about what to destroy next, then suddenly an idea would pop into my head. The next thing I would do would be to rip up the book that was in the cell with me. It was a terrible book by the looks of it, a dreary piece of crime fiction. Page by page, I dismantled the book. It was a spectacular mess, indeed. The next idea I had would be to block the toilet, and so I grabbed all of the paper and stuffed it into the bowl. The room began to flood. You better believe that caused some attention. They treated me like I had a history of violence, or perhaps they thought that I was a danger to myself. The only thing in danger were the items in the prison cell. Everything not fixed to the ground was fair game.

I had succeeded in flooding the room, but I didn't realise that this would affect my sleeping situation. To be fair, sleep was the last thing I wanted to do. I was Kunta Kinte at that moment. I had been captured and taken away from my habitation only to be locked in a cage. It was my instinct to rebel and destroy once my freedom was stolen.

It was a complete contrast to what happened when the police took me from my house. This time, I submitted and was compliant, yet the attitude and aggression did not match the circumstance. My question is whether this was the procedure that they follow with every "mentally ill" person that they detain at the station or did they make an exception for me?

I lost track of time during my stay at the police cell. Minutes seemed like hours. I could not wait to leave this place and go to the hospital. Still, no solicitor was made available. I even requested a lawyer who I knew personally. They told me they didn't get through but who knows if they made the call in the first place? From time to time, the slider on the prison door would open and I would see an officer observing me. All eyes seemed to be on me. As far as I knew, I was the only mentally ill person in that facility.

It dawned on me that anger and frustration would not get me out of this place and that my pleas were worthless. No solicitor was coming either. I decided to change my approach. Let me try to calm down and get some rest. The only problem was that there was water everywhere. It was a mess. The same creative destructive energy I used to flood the place was used to repair. Destroy and rebuild was the mantra. After finding my bearings, I took off my Chicago Bulls top and used it as a soaking instrument. I would squeeze the water I gathered back into the toilet bowl. Before that, I had to unclog the toilet with my hands. I removed that shoddy book piece by piece.

I was cold and topless, but I had to persevere. Eventually, the water level started to visibly diminish, and after an hour or so most of the damage that I had done was cleaned up. The floor was relatively dry, and the toilet unblocked. I was a bit tired now and I decided to try and get some rest. As I laid on the mat, which was still wet, the shivers ran down my spine. A tear dropped down my eyes. I just wanted to help my community. I had to use the wet Chicago Bulls jersey as a blanket. I was shivering and crying inside. The coldness and the wetness of the blue mat were striking. It was uncomfortable and humiliating. I was spiritually broken. This captivity was by far the lowest and most painful experience of my life.

It's hard to imagine that for those in prison, these four walls make up their reality every single day. Once again, the slider on the door opened, and the observation continued. They seemed to be pleased with me sleeping. My submission and compliance must have been reassuring.

I requested a hot beverage and they took pity on me and agreed to provide me with some tea. I was hungry at this point and regretted flushing the food down the toilet.

After what seemed to be an eternity, I received the news that I had been eagerly anticipating. The police had arrived and were going to take me to the hospital. A bed on the ward was now available. In my 25 years on this earth, I had never been happier to see the police. I felt safe in their presence. They were also carrying a more extensive range of equipment than those who came to my house. I asked them about the procedure that led to the Section 136 in the hotel. He mentioned that he might have handled the situation differently. After that, I laid back and enjoyed the ride to the psychiatric ward.

Chapter Five
Ward Life

O nce we arrived at the hospital, they discharged me from the custody of the police to the mental health team. The first thing that caught my eye at Brett Ward was how one of the patients was walking. His movement was sluggish and zombie-like. He was obviously on a high dose of medication. I knew that I had to remain vigilant throughout this experience. I was talking to a doctor about my experiences and this same man approached us. The doctor asked him why he was interrupting us. He offered me some biscuits, as if he somehow knew that I was hungry. The biscuits went down like a treat. He completed some routine tests and declared that there was nothing physically awry. I was a healthy 78 kg with little fat on my frame. I felt great physically and the results of the test reinforced this.

I ate some more food then proceeded with a quick tour of the ward. They showed me the kitchen, lounge, recreational areas, and most importantly, where I would be sleeping. I was eager to get some proper rest and felt relieved to have made it through that nightmarish experience at the police station.

The next morning, I began to evaluate the ward. There was not much to do there, and I quickly grew bored. The television channels consisted of basic Freeview. You would think that they could squeeze the budget and get some TV package, or even Netflix for that matter. The food was pretty good; I must admit, and it quickly became one of the highlights of the day. Breakfast, lunch, and dinner for my well-balanced and healthy palette. There were some books available, but I had no interest in reading any of them. I walked into a small media room. I found a computer with limited internet accessibility, a poor selection of DVDs, and a guitar with a broken string. I had no phone on me and my primary concern was how I would get through the intense boredom I was feeling.

They admitted me to Brett Ward under Section 2 of the Mental Health Act. Section 2 enables the detainment of somebody thought to be suffering from mental illness for 28 days for assessment and treatment. Section 2 is not renewable. However, hospital staff can apply for Section 3. This part of the Mental Health Act enables six months of detention. After the six months are up, it can be renewed for another six months and up to a year at a time. At least, in prison, you know how much time you are going to serve.

You have the right to appeal Section 2 in a tribunal within the first 14 days of admission. As soon as I found out about that right, I submitted my appeal and got the ball rolling. Brett Ward is an open ward where people can voluntarily check themselves in; therefore, the level of security was not that robust.

I was adamant that there was nothing wrong with me. So, when the opportunity arose to escape my captivity, I took it. I left the hospital and had nothing but the clothes on my back, no bus pass or money. The only place I could go was home, and so I began the arduous trek home. I followed the 394 bus home like the three wise men followed the star to find baby Jesus. The journey took about an hour.

The prodigal son had returned, unexpectedly so, which left everybody in the house walking around on eggshells. Before I could even try and process things in my bedroom, the police had arrived to take me back to the hospital. My human right to liberty took a backseat while Section 2 was in place.

They asked me to come with them, and I was adamant that I had the right to remain in my room. My visit to the international slavery museum was still fresh, and I felt like a slave who had escaped, only to be tracked down and dragged back to the compound. Complying with their demands wasn't in my plans. I tensed my muscles to reinforce the fact that I wouldn't go without a fight.

I stood in the middle of the bedroom with the wooden bunk bed to my right and four police officers inching towards me. The radiator that I smashed was to the left of me, and the carpet stains were still present from the incident that led to me being sectioned. My friends and family were stationed near the door, and my best friend recorded the interaction in case things went awry. Once the police realised that contracted muscles are not easy to constrain, they pulled out a Taser. Before I could process the situation, 50,000 volts surged through my body. It was a sensation like no other. In a flash, the contractions of my tensed muscles melted away, and I lost control of my legs. The officers quickly subdued me, and once again, I found myself in handcuffs. It must have been an amateur hour at the police force as the officer who used the Taser on me messed up, and the hook stuck in me after the fact. I needed to be taken to a doctor to remove it before going back to the mental hospital. It was the third time that summer that I entered police custody.

When would this nightmare end? was my immediate thought. I found myself firmly placed in the belly of the beast. We arrived at Brett Ward where the supreme boredom and under stimulation would continue.

Bevan Ward

Upon returning to the hospital, I was deemed too aggressive and unmanageable to stay in the open ward. This resulted in my transfer to the Psychiatric Intensive Care Unit. The first thing I noticed about Bevan Ward was the gym to my left-hand side. That alone surpassed all the so-called recreational activities available in Brett Ward. There was a computer room with working internet, arts, and crafts. A sensory room filled with lights and music, cooking classes, and more. However, there was a schedule for the activities, and it took me a few days to adapt to the system. The gym just seemed so tempting, and I was asking, "Why can't you just open it?" I had been training for 11 years, after all. I couldn't understand why the gym was closed at 2:10 pm when the board says 2:00-3:00pm. It broke my logic. Eventually, I realised that the gym was only accessible if the qualified personal trainer was present. Sometimes, he didn't turn up, even though the gym time was specified. Those sessions were quite therapeutic — even with the limited equipment, that hour of gym time was a precious commodity.

Forced medication is a painful experience to describe. Under Section 2, you cannot resist medication. If you try, then you will be subdued by some big, burly men and injected with medicine in your backside. I hate needles period, and while I hated the idea of taking medicine, I feared the injections more, so I swallowed both my pride and the pills. I witnessed the process happening to another patient and knew that, ultimately, resistance was futile. Compliance was king.

Twenty-eight days is a long time to be assessed and I lost track of the days very early on. There are many ways to get discharged. One of them is a tribunal which coincidentally would take up to 28 days. With great enthusiasm, I made known my desire to go to the court and initiated the process. Within a week, I received a letter from the solicitor confirming that they would be representing me. Communication was difficult as I had an old Nokia flip phone, but I made it work. I was supposed to trade in some credit vouchers for a smartphone, but those plans were interrupted, and I went into the ward vastly unequipped. Constant Internet access would have made the experience more tolerable. My only access to the web was through the allocated browsing sessions that were few and far between.

The TV was a bit bigger than the one in Brett Ward, but it was the same basic package of Freeview. Scrolling between channels trying to find something that would please the majority of patients was an art, and it took some mastering. My fall back option was the music channels, to be honest. I heard, *What Do You Mean?* by Justin Bieber enough times to last multiple lifetimes.

I was like Dr Jekyll and Mr Hyde during the early days of Bevan. When I didn't get my way, a strong feeling of irritation swiftly followed. On one occasion, I landed myself in isolation. After the prison cell experience, the last thing I wanted was containment within four walls. Talking myself into confinement was one of the stupidest things I did during the whole experience. As soon as the door slammed shut, I regretted my decision. I threw a temper tantrum, thinking it would get me out quicker. I did not realise the perception I was giving off. Once I had expelled a sufficient amount of energy slamming down the mattress, I cooled down. I returned from my Hulk-like fury back into Bruce Banner. I talked my way in, and eventually, I managed to talk my way out. The woman behind the glass let me know how my behaviour was being perceived and that I would need to change it if I want to be discharged. I was wise enough to heed her advice. You quickly lose track of time in that place and I vowed never to return there again.

I couldn't understand why some of the people in the intensive care unit were there or what was supposed to be wrong with them. In hindsight, I would have asked how they got sectioned. It was like there was an unspoken "don't ask, don't tell" code when it came to the finer details about our admission.

One of the personalities that stood out was Joshua "The Musician." He was about 6"4', with a muscular build, and he carried a bottle of honey with him at most times. He was Nigerian too, so the cultural connection was there. I was closest to him and he showed me the ropes and told me things that I should and shouldn't be doing. His positivity was captivating. "Give thanks" was his mantra, always grateful to God, despite the circumstance. His voice was also a blessing. I vividly remember the rendition of *What Do You Mean?* that he performed. Unlike the Bieber version, I never grew tired of it.

Another man that stood out was "The Painter." He was very gifted and creative. I had never encountered someone with the ability to visualise something and then so beautifully translate that into a form of art. I get the feeling that he would have become a very wealthy man in the Renaissance era. I purchased three pieces of art from him. Tobacco and of course, old fashioned cash were the currencies in the ward. I think I paid a fiver for one of the T-shirts which he painted on. The image was raw and full of symbolism. He may not have been the most lucid communicator when it came to words but his drawing and paintings said more than a thousand words could.

These two gentlemen were there before my admission. When they discharged me, unfortunately, The Painter was still in the intensive care unit. I do wonder what became of him.

A Turkish gentleman arrived midway through my stay. He had a calm demeanour and seemed to be well connected. He was always ordering pizza and had many visitors. Furthermore, he had a business mind; I recall him receiving a beautiful mountain T-shirt painting from The Painter. He was so impressed that he spoke about how he was going to start selling them.

Another recruit was an older gentleman of Caribbean heritage. Of all people present in the ward, I could not for the life of me understand why this gentleman was locked up. He radiated so much joy that it was contagious. He seemed to find the most pleasure when he was in the sensory room. Lights filled the space and beamed around in a circular, hypnotic pattern. I recall a CD player and an assortment of music to choose between. The seats were very comfortable, and the room did what it said on the tin. It catered for the senses of touch and sound in a very pleasing way.

There was another gentleman who arrived, "Mr Original." His arrival was not like the others. He was very much of the Jekyll and Hyde mould. I remember sitting at the lunch table with him, where he spoke about how we were the original people. He was of African descent and so I agreed. However, he would have these fits of pure rage and would need to be restrained by members of staff. He was pleasant to be around when he was not raging, but you never knew what would set him off, so I maintained a cautious distance from him. We were, however, destined to meet again. One day, as I walked back to my room, which was my only solace at this point, I opened the door and found none other than Mr Original inside my room! This encounter shook me up as I didn't know if he had taken something or placed something there. I had some precious belongings in there, mainly my bespoke pieces of art from The Painter. He left my room without much trouble. That was the last time that I left my door unlocked.

Another noteworthy arrival was The Young One. He looked like he was in his mid to late teens. We did not have many conversations. Still, I do remember me speaking, or instead attempting to engage him with two of my friends who were visiting me. We tried to build some rapport, but even though we were on opposite sides of the table, we were miles apart cognitively. I couldn't understand how he had gotten into this situation. His eyes were vacant as if he was an empty vessel. *What exactly is happening to the young Black men in Hackney?*

CHAPTER SIX

HONOURABLE DISCHARGE

Even though Bevan Ward was larger than Brett Ward, both of these locations were lacking windows. The only real source of sunlight we could get was when the lads stopped outside to smoke their cigarettes. The fresh air felt good but it would be three weeks before I would see sunlight again. Every day, we had this thing called "shop round." It involved a member of staff collecting people's money and going to buy what they wanted from the shops. You definitely didn't want to miss the shop round, as it was one of the few connections to the outside world you could have, besides friends and family visiting, of course. I found comfort in sweet things, biscuits, and fizzy drinks. Towards the end of my stay, I was able to do my own "shop round." I felt like Alice in Wonderland walking to the WHSmith to buy overpriced snacks. Vitamin D on my skin was welcome. Seeing trees, new faces, and books reminded me of life before this whole episode began.

Bevan Ward was the lovechild of prison and school. The baking, computer room, and the arts and crafts reminded me of secondary education. The highly regimented daily schedule was akin to a prison, along with the restricted movement and emphasis on submission. Everything happened on their terms; there was no compromise. I do remember a music session that they held which was pretty cool. I was hesitant to join in but it wasn't like there was anything better to do, so I tried my hand at the guitar and we sang melodies.

By this point, I was accustomed to the ward and was just counting down the days until my tribunal. Before the hearing, however, I was happy to find out that I would finally get to see a doctor. I had been waiting for three weeks for this moment. I was expecting a long, gruelling interview with the specialist. When I finally saw the doctor, he asked me three questions:

1. Do you have any hallucinations?

2. Do you hear any voices?

3. Do you have any thoughts of harming yourself?

I responded no to all of them and before I knew it, he told me he was discharging me. The meeting took less than 15 minutes. I was awestruck, not because of the discharge but because of the criteria that they deem worthy of sectioning. I never had any hallucinations, or heard any voices, or tried to harm myself or others. If that is what counts as psychosis, then why was I given antipsychotics in the first place? However, I did not dwell on that thought for too long because I knew that I was one step closer to getting out of there. I knew in my heart that the moment they put me in front of a doctor, they would discharge me.

I said my goodbyes, packed my bags, and made the transition back to Brett, the open ward.

They say time flies when you are having fun. Unfortunately for me, the 24 hours before my discharge felt like an eternity. It had been almost 28 days, but it felt much longer. I was so anxious to go home, and I was quickly reminded why I was so frustrated with Brett Ward. I tried a variety of things to kill time, eventually settling on reading a book. It was the first piece of literature that I consumed since my admission. The book wasn't great, but it was able to stimulate my imagination and help me ignore my surroundings for a brief moment. I remember one patient who had an uncontrollable tongue; he would stroll up and down the hall shouting all manner of obscenities. I wonder if they admitted him to the intensive care unit. As annoying as I may have been, I know for sure I was not as challenging to manage as he was.

The day had finally arrived; my tribunal would have been in a few days, so it was convenient that the discharge occurred just before then. The doctor, officially at this point, diagnosed me with Bipolar Affective Disorder with psychotic features. I glanced at the paperwork and agreed to every stipulation and assessment he made. Any hesitancy or second-guessing would be construed as lacking insight and would jeopardise my chances of leaving. I had to play ball.

The label stung and hit me like a ton of bricks. The change in perception was immediate.

My first thought was, *What did I do wrong and why did this happen to me?* He stressed the importance of continuing to take the medication and mentioned that I'd have to be on the mood stabiliser for a long time. I said that I would be compliant with the meds. I meant it and also that I had gained insight into my condition. In the back of my mind, I thought, *As soon as I can get off the medication, I will.* They discharged me into the care of the home treatment team. Their role is to intervene and stop people from heading into crisis. They visit your home and supply medication and sometimes watch you take the drugs. He told me to abstain from weed if I was to remain healthy.

Missing Pieces

The ride home on the 394 bus was silent. I was internally happy but you couldn't tell that by looking at my face. My heart was warmed to see the reception that my family had for me. Welcome home signs, banners, and balloons were displayed across the house and in my room. I left them up until they naturally shrivelled up. I felt guilty looking at the state of my room. It had the aura of an abandoned house and many of my belongings were still scattered around. My memory was patchy and I had to rely on others to recall some things that happened during the episode.

My bedroom was desolate. Key documents were missing, along with electronics, and you could tell that the room had been vacant for some weeks. I couldn't for the life of me remember what happened to some of the gadgets that I had. Over my life, I had become a bit of an audiophile and so trying to understand what had happened to the five pairs of headphones I used to own was a monumental task. No matter how hard I tried, I could not remember. People have blackouts after a night out on the town, but this was infinitely worse. I started to wonder if I was actually in control during these moments. Nothing made sense. I remember purchasing a Samsung tablet after being scammed by the two dodgy dealers in Dalston, but there was no recollection of its whereabouts. What else was I forgetting?

The manic summer of 2015 brought a flood of ideas to mind and I naively wrote them down on pieces of paper. Somewhere during the time spent in the ward and various detainments by the police, I lost that piece of paper. I was convinced that those notes contained some concepts that were indeed worth pursuing. But instead, I was lamenting over the loss of the ideas both mentally and tangibly. Some things that survived the purge included some documents from primary school and secondary school, a blue hat, and the £2000 laptop. Letters from the many creditors that I owed money greeted me. Calling creditors was so stress-inducing that my brother tried calling them for me.

My days consisted of three things: I was taking meds, eating, and sleeping. Occasionally, I would browse *The Guardian* to find out what was happening in the world. I also ghosted on Facebook from time to time, and even though I was virtually connecting with these people, it was hard for me to reach out to them and explain what had just happened to me. During my manic phase, I had set up a diversion on my phone. I also couldn't make outgoing calls because I was behind on my phone bills. This meant that incoming phone calls were lost in the ether. Some people must have thought that I dropped off the face of the earth. I would watch Seinfeld as my mother served me a nutritious, heartfelt dinner. As soon as I finished dinner and took the meds, I would be out. It was a struggle to even get out of bed; all I wanted to do was sleep. When I wasn't sleeping, I was reflecting on things. My insecurities were at the forefront of my mind, tormenting me relentlessly.

I was holed up in my room and had no desire to exert myself physically. Despite this, I promised my dad that I would take a walk and get some exercise. Something as simple as that was such a challenge, and I compromised in the end. The local park was about ten minutes away, but it felt like 10 miles. I walked all of thirty seconds to the children's play area adjacent to my house. Gazing upon the estate triggered powerful feelings of nostalgia. My brother had bought me a phone which he gave me during the final days at Bevan Ward. There was no memory card and I only had room for one album at a time. I listened to a few songs from the album, enough so that it would be construed that I was getting a decent walk in. Even though I was not exercising, I was getting some fresh air and listening to music, so I still saw it as progress.

I was in a dark, depressed state — cooped up in my room, stuck in the same routine of eating, medication, and sleep. To get me out of the house, two of my closest friends encouraged me to go for a stroll. We ended up at a local park that played a key role in our formative years. We sat down on the bicycles used for public hire and peddled and reminisced. The pedals spun, but we weren't moving as we hadn't hired the bikes. This, in a sense, represented the current position I was at in life. Spinning my wheels but making no progress. Going over these stories brought a genuine smile to my spirit; however temporary it may have been. Many relationships are fractured, sometimes irreparably as a result of manic behaviour. I said some horrendous things and knowing these guys for as long as I did, I knew what to say to hurt them. These outbursts are one of the aspects of the manic episode that I feel most ashamed about. Despite this, my friends never left my side. They were steadfast during the most tumultuous period of my life.

The Haloperidol, a powerful antipsychotic, was such an inferior medicine that they had to give me another medication to counter its side effects. It quieted my mind and did likewise to my body. My parents saw what it was doing to me, and I could feel the mental and bodily stiffness. The home treatment team would come to my doorstep to deliver medication when I was running low. After two weeks or so, working with the home treatment team, they discharged me to the EQUIP team.

EQUIP is a mental health service that focuses on preventing psychosis. A care coordinator is an individual who has the responsibility of coordinating, facilitating and integrating mental health treatment, care, and support. My first care-coordinator, Angela, visited me in the ward. The experience of talking to her was useful as she had a very empathetic nature. At that point, I wasn't officially an EQUIP service user. An evaluation happened once I was discharged to see if I had indeed had a psychotic episode. My case was borderline, but there was enough evidence to warrant my transfer to the EQUIP team. Angela listened keenly and signposted me to the appropriate services. It was through her that I discovered StepChange, the charity that helps people manage their debts. StepChange would serve as one of the catalysts for me to get my finances in order. Angela also supported my application to be placed on the social housing register; if successful, I would eventually be given a council property and pay heavily discounted rent. Now that I had been institutionalised, the council accepted my application, and I began bidding for properties. I was bidder number 140, so it would be a long wait until I reached position 1.

One of my cherished memories was when Angela invited several service users and me to Winter Wonderland; a Christmas filled experience combining rides, food, and other forms of entertainment. At this point, I spent the majority of my time in my bedroom, but once I found out that Angela would be chaperoning, I decided I would attend. Being in the company of others who had suffered psychotic episodes was helpful as it reminded me that what I experienced was more common than I had assumed. We were all at different stages of recovery, trying to deal with the tricky hands that life dealt us. The adrenaline rush of the roller coaster, as temporary as it was, broke the monotony. I'm glad I went.

A few weeks after transitioning to the EQUIP team, my medication was running low, and I mentioned this in passing. Because it had become a habit to get the prescription sent to my house, the administration error that followed meant that I was without medication for about ten days. I foresaw this happening, and perhaps subconsciously, I didn't reiterate the fact that I was running out of meds because I didn't want to take them anyway. In those ten days without medication, I noticed the stiffness in my body and mind melted away. My thoughts were not as harmful, and I began to research bipolar disorder and the medications that I was taking. I looked at the side effects of the antipsychotics and also studied the difference between Haloperidol and Olanzapine (another antipsychotic medication). I read many stories about people gaining ridiculous amounts of weight. Liver issues and a slowing down of metabolism were also very prevalent. I had noticed a significant amount of weight gain too. Going to the ward at 78 kg and coming out 90kg+. As I continued to read up on the side effect profiles, I swore to myself that I would not retake Haloperidol or any other antipsychotic.

Upon leaving the ward, I was told by a mental health nurse that I'd need to abstain from cannabis if I wanted to avoid relapsing. Like a contrarian child, curiosity got the best of me and I was eager to find out what would happen if I defied the doctor's orders and smoked again. I inhaled deeply and coughed for about a minute straight. Suddenly, memories of the summer rushed back to my head. I had forgotten entirely about the radiator incident. It was scary to think where these memories were coming from and what made me lose them in the first place. When I saw the EQUIP team, I told them that I had stopped the Olanzapine and had started retaking cannabis. They feared I was relapsing and they asked if I would see the home treatment team, and I said yes.

The home treatment team visited me the following evening. I explained the rationale for not taking the antipsychotic. My decision at that point was unchangeable; nothing could sway me, or so I thought. After their repeated attempts to persuade me to take the pills failed, I proceeded to ask them what would happen if I refused to take medicine. The woman casually told me that I would end up back in hospital. Something in my spirit trembled. I interpreted that phrase to mean that if I did not comply with their request, I would be taken back to the hospital. Another interpretation could have been that if I didn't take the medication, my condition would deteriorate and it would eventually lead to me being sectioned again. The thought of going back to that place of boredom, confinement, and torment — so soon after my liberation — was unthinkable. It took me less than a minute of hearing that to change my mind. In the next moment, I swallowed both my pride and the antipsychotic pills.

Despite resuming the medication, I was still unwilling to accept the diagnosis. *There must be a mistake; this can't be me*, I thought. My determination to increase my understanding led to a period of research. I waded through a few documentaries before stumbling upon an article that fit my narrative and helped to feed the doubt that I had regarding the diagnosis. The research paper was titled "Cannabis-Induced Bipolar Disorder with Psychotic Features." Reading this article was the breakthrough I was looking for and it helped crystallise my position. This article describes a college student who suffered from an acute psychotic breakdown due to cannabis abuse which then manifested into bipolar disorder with psychosis. The similarities between our stories were striking.

All documentation that was given to me by the NHS was kept in a green folder. I meticulously studied these records. The diagnosis in the discharge summary was: "Bipolar Affective Disorder, current episode with psychotic symptoms." The label of psychosis suggested that my relationship with reality was impaired. I could accept that proposition, but as I continued to scour the documents, I stumbled upon a piece of information that would serve as the basis for my diagnosis denial.

This document contained information about my history with drugs, my treatment on the ward, but most fascinating was the section that contained information about my mental state on admission:

Mood and Affect: Mood was reported as excellent. He appeared generally elated though with some lability, began crying when speaking about how much he loved his mother.

Speech: Fast and at times difficult to interrupt.

Thoughts: No thoughts of harm to self or others. Thoughts-rapid, some tangentiality on occasions though largely seneschal and easy to follow. Preoccupied with helping others by giving away his belongings, starting projects, etc. Also, how he has changed over the last few weeks, very much for the better. No frankly delusion content. Some religious themes and stated that he is very religious. There were no delusional element to this, however. His main thrust was that Jesus was a metaphor rather than [a] person, and he was living true to this metaphor.

Perceptions: Nil abnormal elicited. Not responding.

Cognition: Grossly intact.

Insight: Low. Appraises his current mental state positively. Does not consider this to be mental illness.

When I read this section, the doubt about my diagnosis multiplied and it would become a cornerstone of my argument against the psychiatrist's judgement. The "treatment of the ward" section also contained some interesting information: "Eché became hostile, irritable, and aggressive in his behaviour. He was unmanageable on an open ward and was transferred to PICU" (psychiatric intensive care unit). I had my perception of how things transpired, admittedly patchy in some places but it was frustrating to read their account of events. Once it's in a report, the information is pretty much treated as gospel.

The doctors do not know what causes bipolar disorder. The only thing that they seem to agree on is that it can be passed down from parent to child. How can bipolar manifest in somebody out of the blue? Especially in someone that showed no symptoms in their childhood. The person in the study and I had one common denominator. Can cannabis cause bipolar disorder? It's a lifelong condition, but if it can spontaneously manifest, then surely, it should be able to disappear similarly?

In this state of mind, it was only a matter of time before I discontinued the medication. Once the home treatment team was off my case, I stopped taking the antipsychotics.

My gym attendance and overall attitude to exercise acted as a barometer for my mood. In times of stability, I would frequent the gym regularly; it was an automatic process. As my mood declined, the frequency would decrease until I stopped going altogether. This cycle played itself out numerous times. I would go from being at the gym for 6 a.m. opening to shrieking at the thought of leaving my house and making the treacherous 20-minute journey. In times of mania or high mood, I would hit the gym six or seven times a week, and sometimes I would go multiple times in the day.

Throughout my years, I developed some unsavoury eating habits and changes in my mental state only magnified this. I went through periods where I was obsessed with "clean eating," and thus, chicken and broccoli became my go-to meal. My relationship with food is a complex one and I think I have danced along the border of body dysmorphia several times. Weight gain was one of the primary reasons for discontinuing the medication.

I liked being lean and it was relatively straightforward getting to a low body fat level, maintaining it was the issue. The weeks of restricting calories would lead to uncontrollable binges, to the point where it felt like I was now a passenger in my own body. Something else would take control and walk to the nearest shop, purchase thousands of calories worth of junk food and scoff it down until my stomach was bloated, and I could no longer move. This unknown force, having known how much damage it had done, would now vacate and leave me to deal with the consequences. I would feel incredibly guilty, and in response, would become even more restrictive in my diet as a form of damage correction. It was, indeed, a vicious circle.

Shortly after being discharged from the home treatment team, I decided to become a personal trainer. I figured I like fitness and it was only going to add a few thousand pounds to my already sizable student loan debt. It was a good experience, and it helped me meet some cool people and also helped me focus my mind on something constructive. Probably most importantly, it injected some much-needed routine in my life. Mania is unexplainably chaotic and this course proved that I was ready for some more responsibility.

The certificate arrived and I began the search for entry-level fitness jobs. It soon dawned on me how oversaturated the fitness sector is. I should have done my due diligence before jumping in. The self-employed model, whereby I would need to pay rent to a gym to train clients, seemed stress-inducing. I flirted with the idea of covertly training clients under the guise of two friends hitting the gym. This plan failed to materialise and I quickly placed the qualification in my back pocket and went searching for another form of employment.

The career trajectory that I was on had entirely veered off course and was now at a standstill. My mood dropped. The people I became accustomed to seeing for the last six weeks were now distant. The messages in the WhatsApp group chat slowed in frequency, eventually grinding to a halt as the thing that united us was finished. In that confusion, I began to think, *Maybe I am bipolar, why else would my mood be changing like this?* So, I started retaking the medication. The vicious cycle that ensued was horrible. The binge eating was back. The demon of greed had consumed me. I regularly fast through the day but I couldn't control it. Everything I ate was in excess, including sweets, biscuits, and peanuts. After each binge, I would swear that this was the last time. I think I lasted about three days before the binge resumed. The comfort that the food would bring was short-lasting as I would look in the mirror afterwards and be disgusted with my reflection.

I was eager to experience something again, and so I scanned through my phone, desperately seeking a cannabis vendor. The tactic didn't work, and so I reconnected with an old school friend who had the desired connections. We met on various occasions, but something was wrong. I felt a strange sensation. Instead of calming things down and relaxing me, thoughts sped up, and I almost felt detached from the present moment. Now that I was no longer under the watchful eye of the home treatment team, I decided that I would yet again discontinue my medication without tapering off. My family discovered that I was smoking still and the tension ramped up. I was a rebel without a cause, and the resentment from being sectioned led me down a familiar path. At this point, I had no source of income and those ideas about debt and declaring bankruptcy had again sprung to mind.

An Einstein-esque idea came to mind. What if I trade the £2000 laptop at computer exchange, declare bankruptcy, and then use the money gained to fund my business ventures? Eager to make this idea a reality, I carefully packed up the laptop and set off for Computer Exchange. The fact that the computer was unbranded meant that the maximum cash figure I could receive was £400. Since I did not plan to pay the debt anyway, I made the trade. Another fantastic business deal was conducted. When I got home, there was a laptop-sized hole in my desk. *Don't worry*, I told myself, *soon your business dealings will take off and you will be able to buy an even better laptop.*

Once my family realised what I had done, they feared the worst. They had been through this nightmare before. After a few weeks, I had spent most of the £400. I was slowly beginning to realise that this was not the best trade. To my surprise, a few weeks later, my brother and mother called me to the living room. My brother firmly gripped a plastic bag. They told me that they had pulled all manner of strings and managed to buy back the laptop that I had traded in. Once I gazed upon the notebook and realised the magnitude of this gesture, my heart sank. It quickly dawned on me how irrational my behaviour was and that my family weren't the enemy. They were just trying to help me and prevent me from spiralling out of control. I was unable to see it as I was viewing life through the lens of mania and psychosis. For the first time in months, I was able to see reality for what it was.

Anxiety and apathy were rife. I didn't know where I was going in life. I saw no light at the end of the tunnel. It was at this point when I told my psychiatrist how I was feeling. They asked me if I wanted to take some antidepressants. I obliged. Between the cannabis, antidepressants, mood stabiliser, and the food binges, I was a shadow of a man. No ambition or hope. I remember being couch-locked and playing video games for hours on end. My only accomplishments were virtual.

I was broke and had just stopped claiming ESA, or Employment Support Allowance. My financial situation was more than precarious, to say the least.

I discovered internet forums around the age of thirteen, and despite the passage of time, I still interacted with them in the same way, always observing from a distance and never posting myself. I visited several online bipolar disorder forums, finding some solace in those digital communities. I had been patient with the antidepressants too. The doctor told me they take about six weeks to kick in.

CHAPTER SEVEN

A BLESSING IN DISGUISE

E very time I smoked, I would suddenly get a rush of negative thoughts. When I wasn't by myself, the negative thoughts were not as prominent. All of my insecurities were instantly at the forefront of my mind. I couldn't explain it, but stubbornly, I refused to give it up. Usually, cannabis would ease my mind and enhance my music listening experience. I tried different strains and methods of ingestion. No dice. My family and friends were telling me about the impact it was having on my life, but I was in full rebel mode. I wanted to prove everyone wrong. There was one occasion when I was smoking with some acquaintances in a park, and it felt like I had disassociated from my body, physically. I was present, but mentally, I was elsewhere.

One of the staff members at EQUIP informed me about a study that was taking place at a prestigious university. After hearing the details, I enrolled in a cannabis trial that provided financial incentives for abstaining from weed. For the first three weeks, I didn't take it seriously and failed the urine tests, receiving no Tesco vouchers. By the end of the third week, I had a change of heart.

I was penniless, and in that situation, every little bit did help. In the next seven weeks, I drastically lowered my consumption and then completely abstained, collecting vouchers every week. I had no problem avoiding it when the incentive was present, but once the study was over, I went straight back to the cannabis. The grip it had over my life was real. I would spend hours trawling through forums reading about the relationship between cannabis and bipolar. There seemed to be two schools of thought. One was that it made things worse and resulted in an increased chance of relapse. The other school of thought saw it as a form of self-medicating. "Everyone reacts to it differently," they said. "It all depends on the strain," others would say.

About five weeks after the abstinence trial, I decided to quit the weed altogether. I had been chasing the high from before, but it just wasn't the same. Caffeine was the next drug to go. At this point, I had lost faith in drugs, period. Legal and illegal. I wanted to find my baseline, in all the madness, I had lost myself. Everything had to go! The great purge.

I decided it was time to start dealing with the debt that I had accrued. There was a stack of letters that I could not bear to open as I feared what the contents would reveal. I mustered up enough confidence to break the seals and see what the damage was. There were dozens of default notice letters. I tallied up the total debt, and even though it was extremely disheartening, at least I could now act to resolve the situation. I called up the creditors and began arranging payment plans. I also wrote to one of them detailing my condition and the fact that I was deemed not to be of sound mind when I made the purchases. I enclosed evidence of my discharge from the NHS and a note from my care coordinator. They wrote back declining my request to have the debt written off. I tried to find out why, but the lady told me that they take each request on a case-by-case basis. It made me wonder what circumstance someone has to be in to get their debt written off. If not for mental illness, then what?

Symbols and Signs

The day had arrived — 26 years in the making. There was no turning back. It was time to make a decision that would alter the course of my life forever. Tears welled up in my eyes as I descended into the waters. One of my favourite songs chorused in the background. I paused briefly and thought about all the events of my life that led up to this moment. I grabbed hold of the pastor's arm, and a few seconds later, I was under the warm water, only to be raised shortly after that.

For most of my life, I was irreligious, hovering somewhere between scepticism and agnosticism. Upon my release from the mental health hospital, I was searching for something to fill the black hole in my soul. It was midday and I was heading to a college open day to find out about a teaching qualification. While waiting for the train to depart from Liverpool Street, I found myself scrolling through the Google Play store, and I stumbled upon the Bible application. I figured I'd give the Bible another chance as my previous attempts had always seemed to fail at Genesis, usually after a few chapters or so. The New Testament scriptures resonated and, before I knew it, I was at Revelations.

To augment my understanding, I would need to find a church and I ended up attending a sermon at a Seventh-day Adventist church. The sense of community was strong and the post-church meals were definitely worth the wait. As Seventh-day Adventists, the Sabbath day (Saturday) is a day of rest and worship and it took a few weeks before I fully integrated this principle. As the weeks passed, my hunger for knowledge and understanding multiplied exponentially. I completed two full readings of the Bible — I was all in. Even at the gym, while attempting to set new deadlifts records, I would be listening to the gospels. In addition to this, to demonstrate my commitment, I threw out my entire music selection, lest I succumb to temptation by secular music.

My perception had changed. I had placed on the religious lens and my worldview, political opinions, and perspective on mental health had shifted drastically. I happened upon scriptures that seemed to show Jesus casting evil spirits out of people.

In the Gospel According to Mark, Jesus encountered a man with an unclean spirit who couldn't be bound with chains, nor could any man tame him. I felt more energetic when I experienced mania, so much so that a handful of officers couldn't restrain me and had to use the Taser. This generous interpretation would serve to confirm my biases.

Matthew 17:15 read, "Lord, have mercy on my son: for he is lunatic, and sore vexed." This line of scripture further entrenched my beliefs. But I had to delve deeper, so I purchased Strong's Concordance, a reference tool that helps identify the common translations of the original Hebrew, Aramaic, and Greek words in the Bible. As much as I did not want to identify as a lunatic, the evidence was insurmountable.

Am I possessed? I thought. I continued to explore this line of thinking. The more I studied, the more it made sense. The medication could be interpreted as a form of witchcraft, and thus taking them would not only be a sin, but it would also demonstrate a lack of faith in God to heal me. I discontinued the medication.

The notion of predestination was tough to comprehend. Had all of our actions already been determined by God? *What does that mean for free will?* I thought. *Did God use this manic episode as a way of drawing me into the faith?*

Confirmation bias led to me tracking down YouTube channels that validated my own opinions. Once I had watched the first couple of videos, the algorithms went to work. Suddenly, I had access to a plethora of Christians who denounced mental health as a form of demon possession and the remedy was purging, repentance, and hard-core prayer sessions.

The religious fervour continued to grow. I was now attending church on Saturday and then Sunday service at a local Church of England parish. I interspersed this with mid-week Bible studies.

I would go on to read the Bible another two times as my beliefs in demons solidified. My theory was that by experimenting with cannabis, I exposed myself to dark spirits from the spirit realm who were now taking up residence inside my body. These evil entities manifested their desires through mania and trying to get me to kill myself via intrusive thoughts and suicidal ideation.

After a ten-month stint, most of my religious zeal had subsided, and I was back to my default mode of operation — sceptical-agnosticism. In the end, it was the doctrine of eternal hellfire that pushed me away from the faith. How could a loving God torture sinners for eternity based on a lifespan of 70 years. It didn't make sense and I couldn't square the circle.

There was still a void that was unfilled, and almost inevitably, I began to veer off into existential and nihilistic depressed stupor. It's at times like this where introspection is truly a blessing and a curse. Getting lost in my thoughts was a regular occurrence, and the negative thoughts would pile up like a pile of bricks, with the same density and gravity. There was nothing to anchor my sense of self to as I sunk deeper into a black hole of emotion, where all matter went to die. Positive thoughts, like light cells, would get sucked into my black hole, never to be seen again. The weight of the diagnosis hampered my rational thinking faculties, and I felt resentful and persecuted. Why me? Life was already full of strife before the diagnosis, how on earth would I make anything out of myself?

I was made aware of a course that was taking place in East London. A teaching qualification that enables individuals to lecture in further education environments, working with students aged 16 and over.

I was very hesitant when it came to deciding whether to enrol. After qualifying as a personal trainer, was I about to jump in and do yet another training course? I felt slightly coaxed into registering by my mother, who convinced me that it was an excellent qualification to have. I didn't know what to expect; yet, once I turned up for the first lesson, I was disappointed at the lack of professionalism. It seemed I had a penchant for attracting dysfunction.

All of the progress that I had made while studying to become a personal trainer was gone. I was around 95 kgs at this point and feeling despondent. I remember weird thoughts beginning to emerge. I would be heading to college, and I would look at the oncoming train, and feelings would come into my mind saying, what if...? The same would happen as I approached the college and walked past the river, that same idea saying, why don't you just end it? Throughout this whole experience, I had never experienced suicidal ideation to this level.

It was at this point, something impressed upon me to stop taking all medication. I went the extra mile and gathered all my medication, even emergency meds, and threw them in the garbage. It was an act of faith. Let's get down to the bottom of this. I had had enough of the suicidal thoughts and weight gain. The medical professionals always warned me not to stop abruptly, but to wean off the meds slowly. I went cold turkey overnight. One way or another, we would find out if I was indeed bipolar. I decided it was time to put my PT qualification to practise. I was my first and only client at the time. Twelve weeks of vigorous training and calorie counting led to me going from 94 kilos to 79 kilos. The fat simply melted off. "The meds don't affect your weight; it only makes you hungry." Yeah, right! I felt like myself again as things began to fall into place. I was feeling creative and ambitious. Nothing had changed from my previous attempt to lose weight. It was the same intensity and diet; the only variable that changed was coming off the meds.

The college was not very organised when it came to helping students secure a college placement. Luckily, I was able to secure an internship at a school/sixth form college in North West London. I was able to gain insight into lesson planning and classroom management. I was in the English department incidentally, where I felt some words push to the forefront of my mind. I saw that the teacher had everything under control, and so I began scribbling the words down: "The Matrix is real / The news just conceals / The truth when revealed / First stings, then it heals."

The school was quite strict when it came to the staff uniform. I hated ties since my introduction to them in secondary school. They seemed pointless and needlessly constricting. Despite this, I bit my tongue and wore the uniform until the end of the term. Upon reaching that checkpoint, a meeting with the principal to loosen up the dress code would occur.

One fateful afternoon, I was participating in a drama class, and I decided to remove my tie so that I could fully immerse myself in the experience. The session was great, and the young people seemed to enjoy it. A figure emerged in the distance during one of the intervals. It was my supervisor. He caught my eye and most importantly, my tie-less neck. The next day was the final day of half term, and after my session had finished, my supervisor called me into the office. He mentioned that he saw me without my tie and brought my character into question. I reacted defensively and made my case.

My tone of voice was more aggressive than usual and I was visibly aggrieved. Familiar energy coursed through me. My supervisor gave me the option to go back to my lesson and continue the discussion later when cooler heads prevailed. I decided this was the best moment to put my foot down and declared that if I did continue, I would not be wearing my tie, in protest. At that moment, I knew my time at the school was over. I wasn't sure if I quit or if he fired me, but we both knew that this was the end of my tenure. I took my leave with my tie in hand. Once the dust had settled, the confusion overwhelmed me: Why had I given up a position that I genuinely enjoyed? The young people were hilarious, and every day was rich with intrigue and surprises. Was the tie that big of a deal and why was I so aggressive? I didn't feel like myself. Suddenly discontinuing medication can lead to a swing in mood, and this incident had the hallmarks of hypomania, the milder version of mania.

Chapter Eight
WELL EQUIPPED

One of the activities that I was referred to by my care coordinator was the tree of life. An assembly of individuals who had suffered a psychotic episode who would use this activity as a means of reflection and establishing a better sense of who they were. I went in with an open mind and was happy to share my experiences. Everybody in that room was at a different stage in their recovery process, so they would share as much as they felt comfortable. That tree of life session made me think about my roots and my values — family, friends, and those that lie somewhere in-between. The branches represented the different things I had accomplished, and as much as it was a cathartic process, it was also an eye-opener as I realised that I hadn't done nearly as much as I would have hoped. The fruits would represent the things you wanted to do in the future. One of my terrible habits is comparing myself to others. This is a bad trait during regular times, let alone after suffering a major manic episode. The worst example of this was when I would log onto LinkedIn to see how those I went to university were doing.

LinkedIn's visual CV would display as much detail as the individual deemed necessary, so I would see the transition from one fortune 500 company to the next. Furthermore, the levels of experiences and stability were disheartening. X number of years in the same job and progressing steadily into a position of seniority. What was I doing? As I completed the tree of life exercise, the feeling of inadequacy flowed through every cell in my body. Even though each individual has had a different card dealt to them, the comparisons were inevitable. It was a harmful habit that needed breaking, but to do so, I would have to reorient my thinking.

For unknown reasons, Angela, my first care coordinator, shortly departed. But before she left, she referred me to a counsellor. I was initially hesitant, but I tried to keep an open mind and thus signed up for a 10-week course. The first few meetings enabled me to regurgitate as much of the episode as I could remember with the therapist furiously scribbling down notes.

As the weeks progressed, we moved from discussing the details of the incident and instead tried to identify the potential triggers. The service was cognitive behaviour therapy, and so ideally, I would be developing psychological tools and skills that would enable me to navigate extreme mood fluctuations. She compiled an extensive list of potential triggers and sent it to me for my perusal. My therapist was pregnant and went on maternity leave before our sessions finished; thus, a new counsellor would have to take over. At this point, I was reluctant to be as open to the new therapist. It was a delicate balance of sharing information but not giving too much away as I was scared of what the implications could be.

I was assigned a temporary care coordinator. Another female by the name of Karen. Unlike Angela, she was a Black woman, and so there was less cultural distance. Her approach was different to Angela's but very useful, nonetheless. At this point, I had gone into a depressed state, and my gym activity had ceased. Karen managed to reorient my thinking and helped me understand that the person who was at the gym for the opening bell was still in there somewhere and that if I could somehow unlock it my passion for fitness could once again manifest. Her contract was short term, but luckily, her role was extended, and she was with me for just over a year. I felt very safe confiding in her, and I eventually let her know that I had discontinued my medication because I felt guilty withholding such vital information.

These care coordination sessions with Karen acted as quasi-therapy sessions as I would unload with whatever thoughts and anxieties that were ruminating. The EQUIP service referral lasted for three years, after which, I would transition to a team that offers less frequent contact. One of the good things about the EQUIP team is that the care-coordinators adapt to where the client is in their journey. At times when I was doing better, I would see them less frequently. However, when my mood dropped, I would see my care-coordinator weekly.

The dreaded day finally came. Karen told me that she was leaving. I knew the day would come, and I was due for a third care coordinator in two years. Building up the rapport and trust would take time, and I considered closing myself off to whoever would replace Karen because it was unlikely that we would connect in the same way.

When I transferred to the EQUIP team, I was sent a brochure for Core Arts, a non-profit that promotes positive mental health and wellbeing through creative learning. I glanced at the leaflet, but the activities didn't appeal to me — the timetable contained an assortment of music and art sessions, from live band jam sessions to piano lessons. I placed the booklet back in the letter and buried it in a folder where I kept all documentation on my mental health. After writing my first piece of poetry, I continued to dabble, and the more I wrote, the better I felt. What's interesting is that before being sectioned, my attempts at writing poetry always fell flat. After the manic episode, writing now served a cathartic and therapeutic purpose. Instead of storing thoughts in my head, I was able to download them onto pieces of paper. In addition to this, the writing served as a time capsule of sorts. It would capture where I was emotionally, mentally, and spiritually at whatever time it was when I wrote each piece. I spoke to my care coordinator and asked for a referral to Core Arts. An invitation was made to an open day to check out the different facilities.

There is an association between bipolar disorder and creativity. It's often romanticised in popular culture. In my experience, there was such a rapid shift in creativity and the desire to express myself that it's hard not to associate it with the condition; perhaps it is a side effect.

Recent cuts to charity funding meant that new referrals to Core Arts were limited to one year's access. I wanted to make the most of this opportunity, and since I wasn't working at the time, it provided an excellent chance to get out of the house. The open mic jam session I began attending was great; it was a mix of ethnicities, musical styles, and age demographics. What united us was our experiences of ill mental health. I cherished these moments where we could just get lost in the music, make mistakes, and express our innermost feelings through music and lyricism. I attended the weekly sessions and performed a few times at the monthly Core Arts showcase. The positive side effect was an increase in confidence and 2017 was a very creative year for me. I frequented many open mic nights in conjunction with my Core Arts endeavours. There really seemed to be a strong correlation between my creative output and my mood.

However, 2018 was a year dominated by depressive mood states and I followed my newly established all-or-nothing, zero-sum game pattern. I went from attending weekly open mic nights and performing multiple times in a month to not penning a single lyric or attending any open-mic nights. The quest for balance would continue.

The last care-coordinator I would have was Desmond, of Irish persuasion. He had a great deal of experience and a pleasant demeanour. It took a few weeks for me to begin opening up. The common thread between the three care-coordinators is that they gave me agency when it came to decisions regarding my treatment. I could be honest with them if I felt like a particular medicine was not working well. It did take a while for me to understand that they were not trying to section me but instead, they were trying to prevent me from relapsing. Once I had grasped this, I was more transparent, and I cycled between a few mood stabilisers before finally finding one that agreed with me and had few if any side-effects.

Desmond was always very encouraging when I told him of my plans. At this point, I had begun working for an alternative provision secondary school to work with young people who weren't in mainstream education. It was part-time work, but it was one small step back into the working world. It was a tough job, and the emotional baggage was often overwhelming. I tried to keep positive energy, even if it was just a façade, particularly during periods of low moods. Despite my best efforts, it was hurting my performance, and I felt like I was operating beneath my potential. I avoided taking mental health days off because I wanted to be a consistent presence in my student's lives.

When I told Desmond about my desire to use my DET qualification and try and secure a lecturing position in a college, he gave me nothing but encouragement. I wondered how my diagnosis would mesh with the demands of the teacher, who according to numerous anecdotes, were overworked and overstressed. People were leaving the profession in droves. Was I walking into a situation that could trigger another episode of mania? I made my reservations known, but Desmond assured me that if I implemented the knowledge and tools that I had developed, I could make a success of it. I decided to do a bit of research, hoping to find examples of high-functioning teachers with a bipolar disorder diagnosis. I stumbled across numerous forums and articles which had the opposite effect. The vast majority of the posts told stories of short-lived careers and exits from the teaching profession. The seeds of doubt were beginning to bear fruit.

Despite my reservations, I applied for a handful of lecturing positions, rejecting the temptation to make generalisations of the teaching profession based on a few anecdotes. It was spring 2018, and I had almost spent three years working with the EQUIP team. Unless the condition of the individual has deteriorated, eventually, they'd be transferred to a less intense and specialised team. Upon glancing at the handover date, I was immediately brought back to my first encounter with the mental health service. Things had come full circle. It was akin to graduation, and over the last three years, I was made aware of tools, resources, and services that I could draw upon in times of crisis.

One of the colleges that I applied for had responded and invited me to an interview. I thought my performance was decent, and on the train ride home, I began to question once again whether or not I could handle the rigours of teaching. One terrible anecdote led to the other, and the anxiety steadily increased. I gave up looking for positive stories of high-functioning teachers with bipolar disorder. I was pleasantly surprised when the phone call came in offering me the position.

Once I left the EQUIP team, I would have to be proactive in applying these resources and even more importantly being honest and accountable to myself. I was happy to give Desmond the news that I had accepted a lecturing position, and he commented on the journey I had been on. He had seen me during my darkest hours and was now witnessing an upwards trajectory. The last psychiatrist that I spoke with informed me about a mood stabiliser that I had not yet tried. It was called Lamotrigine. I made a note and then read up on the side effects once I got home. I was pleased to read that the weight gain side effect that often caused me to cease my medication prematurely did not occur with Lamotrigine. The doctor was soft-spoken and empathetic and of all the psychiatrists I have encountered, he was the one who made the lasting impression. The lithium didn't sit well with me, and the Sodium Valproate seemed to dull my senses too much. I tried to temper my expectations as we began the slow titration of the Lamotrigine medication. We started with small doses and scaled up every two weeks. I didn't have an increased appetite, and there were no signs of weight gain.

On the contrary, it seemed to be helping me lose weight to a small extent. One of the complex aspects of mental ill-health is medication administration. There are aspects of trial and error, and while I was in the hospital, it felt like I was a guinea pig for the doctors to test out different cocktails of medications. Different individuals will respond to the same medications differently, and the side effect profile could be wholly dissimilar. Fortunately for me, I had found, in Lamotrigine, a drug that I could consistently take for the long term.

My final day with the EQUIP team had arrived. I would miss the advice of the care coordinators. I had opened myself up in a very intimate manner, and I did not feel that I could do the same with the new service. I gave Desmond a firm handshake and thanked him for everything he had done. He wished me the best and gave me a final word of encouragement. The binary notion of good and bad when it came to the mental health "system" was well and truly shattered. There are good, genuine people working in the system who want the best for you — my interactions with the system before I was hospitalized and those after were markedly different. My paradigm had shifted, and it dawned on me how much agency I had.

By this point, I was no longer under the care of the EQUIP team, and I was working with a care coordinator who I seldom saw. After a few months of conflicting schedules due to my working hours, to prevent wasting resources, I was discharged and referred back to my GP. This was a good sign, I guess, but this seismic change would require me to develop a whole new level of personal accountability, honesty, and the ability to draw upon all of the lessons I had learned on this journey. Unlike in 2015, I had the benefit of diagnosis and prior events to draw upon. The behavioural patterns were known to me, and if I was proactive enough, I could hopefully address the rises and dips in the mood before they become destructive. The goal now was to find a balance and no longer exist in a world full of polarities. I had failed thus far to achieve this — yo-yo dieting and shifting my weight from lean to fat, then fat to lean in what seemed to be an inevitable cycle.

One of the toughest aspects of mood fluctuations is that some of the ideas and projects that emerge during mania show potential. Unfortunately, once the high of the mania wears off, the doubt and disbelief floods back in. The progress that was made comes to a crashing halt and all momentum is lost. It's hard to gain traction again, and I begin to wonder whether it was even me in control. The wonders of technology provide the ability to look at the posts I made, the photos I have taken, and the things I recorded during these moments of mania. I distinctly recall discovering that Google had uploaded the images that I took during the manic episode to their cloud servers. These photos told a thousand stories and helped to fill in some of the gaps in my memory.

Reflecting on the snaps that I took was a bittersweet experience because I was just reliving the experience in a digital format. I saw the manifestation of my elevated mood initially through positive behaviours. I was spending more time with my family, reconnecting with old friends and trying to develop more meaningful connections. I was taking time to appreciate the beauty of life and capturing beautiful shots of nature and architecture steeped in history. As the pictures continued, it revealed how my behaviour became more and more erratic. I took many cloud photos, fixated with the skies, the heavens, and everything else in the cosmos. I felt this oneness or connection to the universe, and whenever I glanced up at the sky, I felt like God was smiling down.

There were also photos of the random items that I purchased, none of which I possessed to this day. As I stared fixedly at this time capsule, I saw that there was a method to the madness. The pictures I took at the slavery museum in Liverpool reflected this. An image full of piles of black bags filled with clothes reminded me of the urge to purge and downsize. These things made sense, and I couldn't help but wonder where it all went downhill. The descent into chaos continued until the final picture, taken in September 2015. A few days after taking that last photo, I was sectioned.

Things could have turned out so different. How would events have played out if I had avoided cannabis? What would my fate have been had I avoided sectioning? My mind was able to conjure up all manner of scenarios and alternative universes. I took solace in those daydreams, living vicariously through them until I ultimately came crashing back down to this unfortunate reality.

I opened my computer and the mouse cursor began moving violently without me interacting with the laptop. After a few minutes of inspection, I discovered that the laptop touchpad was faulty and if I controlled the mouse with it, it was only a matter of time before the cursor would start to move by itself. To test my hypothesis, I connected my USB mouse and completely disabled the laptop touchpad. The problem was solved. No, it wasn't the government or GCHQ remotely accessing my computer; it was just some faulty hardware on a £2000 laptop. I wanted to find my warranty and file some sort of complaint with the manufacturer, but I couldn't summon enough energy to do so.

At the height of my mania in 2015, I was posting updates on Facebook with alarming regularity. I hesitate to think of some of the things I would have been saying. My default state is to watch and observe the different interactions and debates that occur in comment sections. Deep in the dark corners of Facebook is a section reserved for messages sent by people who are not your friends. I stumbled across this section quite randomly but what I saw astounded me. Somebody had reached out because they had found the wallet I lost in Liverpool.

I contemplated taking legal action in an attempt to redress the injustice that I had undergone. I was particularly aggrieved at the tasering. Following a short spell of research, I decided against contacting human rights lawyers. I saw myself as a small cog and trying to take on a colossal institution was a lost cause. I needed another outlet to channel my anger.

At this point, I had mustered up the confidence to begin talking about my experiences in a public forum. I ran several workshops titled "Mental Health & The Black Community: Prison By Another Name?" The attendees included mental health service users, concerned family/friends, practitioners, community activists, and those interested in the topic. These sessions allowed me to vent my frustration more productively. The pain from the sectioning was still quite fresh, and this reflected in the delivery of the workshops. Things were definitely framed in an "us v. them" dynamic. Only time would enable me to develop a more nuanced perspective on the events that occurred.

Assembling that cross-section of people was fascinating as there were many different worldviews on display. I felt that I had an interesting perspective to share, as a young Black male who had seen the good, the bad, and the ugly within the system. I distinctly remember the first workshop not going to plan at all. I was hoping that people would be willing to open up about their mental health struggles, but when I opened up the floor, it was close to radio silence. I needed to say something, and before I knew it, I was giving an account of my experience of mental health. I spoke for an hour straight. What struck me was the fact that so many people in attendance could relate to what I was saying. I assumed that my experiences of detainment and forced medication were particularly unique. Certain cultural factors have prevented honest conversations about mental health and only served to heighten the feeling of stigma. By giving these talks and conducting the workshops, I was doing my part to reduce the stigma. The first few sessions were strange as I was revealing specific details of my life that I wasn't very comfortable doing. As I continued to conduct the events, however, I worried less about the stigma, partly because of the feedback that I was given by others who were encouraged by my honesty and willingness to speak out on these critical issues.

I ran one of my workshops in partnership with MIND in Haringey. Some good connections emerged as a part of that. Upon completing the session, I completed the two-day mental health first aid training. This training gave a good overview of common mental health conditions, the signs, symptoms, and potential ways to mitigate and handle precarious mental health scenarios. In addition to this, I was featured in BBC and Channel 4 mini-documentaries about mental health. It's weird, but I recorded both of these documentaries which were separated by at least ten months when I was in a depressed and darker state. As a result of this, I haven't watched the documentaries as it's hard to watch myself in that particular frame of mind. I do not regret putting myself out there and I would say that it was a significant step in reducing the stigma that I felt. Once something is on the internet, there is no real way you can erase that activity from cyberspace. I had accepted that reality but the diagnosis was still up in the air.

While I was promoting one of the events on Facebook, a gentleman got in touch with me and asked if I recollect visiting his vinyl store and if I had left anything there. Slowly but surely, my mind began to access fragments of lost memories. *The tablet that I bought during the height of my spending spree; is this what he is referring to?* I told him that I would be straight down. I rushed down to the shop and anxiously waited as he rummaged upstairs in search of a messenger bag that I had left. Despite his best efforts, he did not find it. However, he did mention that his colleague may have known where it was. I came back a few days later and his colleague emerged.

There it was, in all its glory, my brown and blue messenger bag. I thanked both of them for their kindness and reflected on the randomness of the encounter. If I hadn't run that workshop and paid for Facebook promotion, I would never have entered the newsfeed, and I would have never remembered what happened to the tablet and my messenger bag. The contents of the bag were interesting and each item told its own story. The Samsung tablet and a packet of antidepressants were in the bag — relics of the manic episode.

From my time in the ward, two characters had made a lasting impression. Joshua, the Nigerian musician, and The Painter. On the way to an art therapy workshop, I spotted a figure whose face bore a striking resemblance to The Painter. As I closed the distance, I realised that it was him. *I wonder if he remembers me?*

I crossed the road, and before I could speak, he greeted me and asked how I was doing. I said that it was good to see him out, and before we departed, he stated that I should have never been in the ward. This comment vindicated my denial and scepticism of the mental health service. He was in a hurry and so the encounter soon came to a close.

Sometimes, I wonder about the small things that lead to chance encounters. There are so many variables that have to synchronise to facilitate these meetings. I was on the bus heading home after an uneventful evening. The driver announced that we had to leave the bus as it had developed a fault. I complied and waited for a few minutes before continuing my journey. I was standing on the lower deck with my phone in hand. A figure descended from the upper floor. I recognized the hairstyle. It was Joshua. We exchanged details in the ward, but whenever I tried ringing him, it went straight to voicemail. I didn't expect to see him again, and so this was a delightful surprise. We spoke for a couple of minutes and his stop quickly approached. I got off before my stop because there was so much to catch up on. We stood on the pavement for just over an hour, reminiscing and exchanging stories. Before we departed, I made sure that I had his correct contact details. We agreed to meet up in the next few weeks for a proper catch-up.

I met up with Joshua a few times over the following months. First, we met at a bar and then we had another chance meeting at the gym which turned into a joint workout. A few weeks after the session, Joshua called me, and I agreed to meet for some drinks at the Ace Hotel in Shoreditch. Something was off, and I couldn't put my finger on it. His interactions with the public were off-kilter and more intense than usual. His mannerisms were different from what I was accustomed to seeing. It wasn't a particularly enjoyable meeting and I wrote it off an anomaly. A few months passed before I spoke to Joshua again. He had been readmitted to the hospital. It appeared that our encounter took place during an episode. This is what my family and friends must have felt like, multiplied by a factor of 10.

CHAPTER NINE

WAR AND PEACE

Depression is akin to a toxic relationship. An individual who does nothing but suck the energy from you. It is made worse by this individual having in-depth knowledge of your insecurities, worries, and failures. These deficiencies were regularly highlighted and served no other purpose than to destroy my self-esteem. The colour in life was removed by this partner of mine who had a very nihilistic outlook on life. It was this same pessimism that made previous passions seem pointless. She wanted me all to herself, and thus, I cut myself off from the world and basked in despairing solitary confinement, expertly erecting facades to get me through the day. Depression is a trained actor, and they made me adept at hiding what I was truly feeling and regurgitating an automatic response of "I'm doing alright, you know," whenever asked, "How are you?" She took me to the precipice and encouraged me to end it all, delivering a persuasive argument that by no longer existing, I would no longer be a burden to my family and friends.

Mania, on the other hand, is an alluring temptress — charismatic, charming, and irresistibly seductive. She builds me up and convinces me that I can do no wrong, encouraging me to chase my dreams and live for the moment. As inhibitions decrease, this, of course, leads to reckless behaviour. That friend that your parents warned you to steer clear of because they would get you into trouble and then flee, leaving you to face the consequences. It was mania who encouraged me to rack up all the credit. At the beginning stages, everything seems to be going well. There's never a dull moment when she's around, and in her shadow comes an abundance of ideas, lyrics, and concepts to explore. Her unrelenting energy oozes and ultimately energises me, giving me a laser-sharp commitment to whatever goal I set for myself, be it social, business, or other projects.

I was due to start work in August 2018 before the academic year commenced, but because of my diagnosis, I needed medical clearance. Administration problems meant that I would ultimately begin in October. Not the most promising start to the new position. I would have to hit the ground running. I had already handed in my notice, and the three months that I waited for my clearance were painful. I was sitting idly, watching my savings depreciate. An idle man is a devil's workshop, and I had nothing but time to ruminate and vividly imagine all the horrible ways in which I would fail. Second-guessing my decision was inevitable, and the confidence in my abilities decreased with each passing day. Ultimately, my desire to avoid a "what if" scenario enabled me to press on and commence with the lecturing role.

This would be my first full-time job since the diagnosis. I performed sufficiently and the plan was to go from strength to strength while pursuing my hobbies and passions. I adapted reasonably well, and the more experienced staff were happy to pass on best practice and help me find my feet. There were instances where I had to dig deep into the reservoirs of resilience to keep myself going. The façade of composure and confidence was close to slipping. With time, I managed to navigate fluctuations in mood, riding the highs and surviving the lows.

I understand why 20% of teachers plan to leave the profession within two years. Teaching is a difficult job under normal circumstances, but battling bipolar disorder only compounds the difficulties. There were indeed testing days; sometimes the pep was absent in my step, and it became tough to mask it. The frequent half-term breaks always seemed to crop up at just the right time.

Despite now being qualified to teach in colleges, I was wholly unprepared for working with inner city students. My classroom lacked authority. Partly because I was scared of them and also because I thought that if I was lenient then they would like and accept me. Agreeable, like all personality traits, can be counterproductive when taken to extremes. I was too agreeable and the students were street smart and savvy. They knew how to identify the boundaries and push them. I gave them an inch and they took three miles.

In the classroom, I overheard students and sometimes colleagues making reference to X teacher as bipolar, in a clearly pejorative tone. I didn't take it to heart but those incidents did make me hesitate to disclose my condition, lest I be subject to stigma and a change in how people perceived my actions.

I left college after a challenging day at work, visualising my bed and trying to decide what TV drama would help me unwind. I boarded the train as per usual and turned on my noise-cancelling, commute-saving headphones. The journey was routine to me at this point; having completed it over dozens of times, I was fully acclimated and had it down to a science. I was immersed in an audiobook when it dawned on me that the train had been motionless for an extended time. I glanced at the window and saw numerous figures walking down.

Something felt wrong. After removing my headphones, I looked around the carriage and was greeted by a sea of exasperated and annoyed faces. An announcement began. The worst-case scenario had materialised. The speaker echoed as the announcer revealed that somebody had committed suicide. The voice told us to leave the train as they had shut down the grid to tend to the poor soul that had jumped onto the tracks.

I've experienced delays because of somebody jumping onto the tracks, but I had never been on the train where the actual incident occurred. The anger melted away and the grim aura of death radiated. We were waiting as they opened the doors carriage by carriage. We walked down the platform towards the front of the train; curiosity led me to glance at the emergency team who had pitched up a forensic tent on the track. It was a weird feeling as the reality that someone had just lost their life began to settle in. At the same time, my thoughts were of how I was going to get home that night.

After three years of bidding for council properties, I was now in the top 2, which meant that I would be invited for viewings. On a cold February afternoon, I went to visit a property 7 minutes away from the family home. A one-bedroom flat on the fifth floor. It was perfect. However, because I was number 2, I would only get the property if number 1 declined to accept. After being shown the kitchen and bathroom, I resigned myself to failure. Surely anyone would accept such a promising council flat in central London. Then the woman who was ahead of me in the queue stated that she was declining the property. She was expecting a baby, so the fifth floor was a big hindrance. Still in disbelief, I collected the keys from the council worker.

A friend who I had worked with on a couple of projects had found himself on the wrong side of the mental health system. Visiting him in hospital for the first time was strange as I found myself on the other side of the visiting experience. Inevitably, images of my time in the hospital ward rushed to my mind. The feeling of gratitude at not having returned to the hospital was nullified by the knowledge that my friend had been there for ten months, with no expected date of discharge.

I noticed a pattern had begun to emerge whenever there was a break in the academic year, and things would quickly spiral down for me. It happened in February, April, and the May half term. All semblance of routine would collapse, and I would fall into a depressed state. The projects that I would be pursuing would lose all momentum. Once the summer holidays arrived, I visualised a productive summer where I would invest my time in getting these projects off the ground. Within the first two weeks, it appeared that the pattern would continue. I lost focus, became pessimistic, and the four walls of my bedroom became my prison cell. How on earth could I live a life like this? No stability and no continuity. However, as the third week began, things started to pick up. My energy increased and my gym usage was automatic. The productivity was terrific and I felt compelled to revisit projects that I was unable to get off the ground because of dips in mood. The desire to connect with family and friends increased along with my level of gregariousness. It had all the hallmarks of mania, but I felt like I was in control. Now, I doubted myself because this is what a manic person would say to themselves. The impulsivity even reared its ugly head via reckless spending.

Most of the doubt regarding my diagnosis would fall away as I seemed to fit the criteria for mild mania, otherwise known as hypomania. What if this isn't mania but a result of conscious efforts to develop my personality? And on that point, how malleable is one's personality? Is it not feasible that I managed to embrace my extroverted nature? The etymology of the word persona has Latin roots, and it means a mask or the character played by an actor. Was I acting out a brand-new role? Perhaps a psychotic episode was round the corner and I would be keeping my friend company in the hospital ward soon enough. I guess only time would tell. Bipolar disorder was a parasite that had merged with my personality, muddying the waters and leaving me wondering whether I should take responsibility for my actions during mania. How would I know when I was losing control? The most pervading question is simply; "Where does bipolar disorder end and where do I begin?"

After seven months of riding high, my mood took a sharp dip. One of the coping mechanisms I adopted was to track my mood daily via an application. It was helpful to visualise the trends and also to see what activities correlated with the most favourable states of mind. It felt like the rug had been pulled from under me. I had put all of these plans in motion with the workshop and the book on the horizon. The deadlines were looming, but the optimism was absent. I could not emotionally connect with the projects that I had been involved in. It was almost like an external force had taken over my body and carried me to this point, and now I was back in the driver's seat, filled with confusion and fear.

What if I hadn't made as much progress as I'd imagined? Perhaps the optimism and renewed energy were down to hypomania. I tried not to engage the thought, but the mere hint that it could be true rattled me to the core. I thought I had escaped the cycle of extreme mood fluctuations once and for all.

My bed provided a few hours of reprieve from the intrusive thoughts. Upon waking on a Monday morning, I decided that enough was enough. I had put up a good fight, but the battle was lost. Down the escalator, I went. I had my headphones in my bag but I had conceded to the intrusive thoughts, and thus I didn't even bother turning my headphones on in an attempt to drown out the negativity. Within a few minutes, I had reached my destination. In a conciliatory tone, I greeted the pharmacist and asked for a repeat prescription of the mood stabiliser, Lamotrigine. It had been a few months since my last prescription. The rise in my mood correlated with the period when I discontinued the meds. It couldn't be a coincidence, the pattern was there for all to see, but my ego couldn't bear to admit defeat. I wanted to do it my way and prove to the world that the diagnosis would not hinder me.

My request was administered, and I left the pharmacy, hoping that there wouldn't be any processing issues. The next day, I returned, paid for my prescription, and headed home. I placed the packet of pills on the table and examined the label. Up until now, I had never entirely accepted the diagnosis. The sense of doubt diminished, but I still flirted with the prospect of a misdiagnosis. My backup tactic was to attribute the psychotic episode to substance misuse. I placed the packet of Lamotrigine on the desk and headed to the kitchen to pour myself a glass of water.

The war was finally over, I finally accepted that the diagnosis was accurate, but the power to control my life's trajectory was still in my hands. Living a fractured existence was unsustainable, and at this point, I realised that despite my constant denials, I do have bipolar disorder. What I wouldn't do is let that define me. I made peace with the fact that I might need medication for the rest of my life. More significantly, perhaps, was the acceptance that within me exists the potential for manic episodes and the potential for depressed states. I can try my best to minimise the fluctuations, but at the end of the day, change is inevitable. Resisting the diagnosis and looking at the manic episode as something extrinsic and separate from me led to a lack of accountability. At the end of the day, it was me who racked up the debts, gave belongings away, and created numerous works of art. The reason that I struggled to understand where the bipolar disorder ends and where I began was that the two cannot be separated. It seems that I had to be completely broken in two to experience a greater sense of wholeness.

Integrating these two states was a significant step in the quest for identity. Time is one of the best healers, and with it also comes clarity. As cliché as it may sound, if I could go back, there's nothing I would change because the resilience that has been borne from these trials and tribulations has pushed me to greater heights. Yes, the black hole of depression is devastatingly debilitating, but I can draw upon the many coping strategies that I have learned along the road. Also, I have the benefit of having gone through what I went through, and now I understand the signals and triggers.

Bipolar disorder was like a symbiote in the way that it had wrapped around my personality and my identity. The bond was so strong that it became impossible to separate me from the illness. My persona existed somewhere in between the mania and the depression. Hypomania seemed to supercharge the best aspects of myself, whereas depression turbocharged all of my worse traits. Both mood states distort the lens from which I viewed reality and the events that unfolded. I would make some progress, gain some stability and start looking towards the future. And in this state of mind, the same thoughts would begin to creep in. Maybe I'm not bipolar after all, perhaps they misdiagnosed me and it would culminate with the notion that I need to get off the medication. I didn't need much of an excuse to taper off the drugs. In one instance, I called it an experiment, and in another, it was construed as an exercise that I needed to undergo to find myself because my sense of identity was blurred.

Once upon a time, I thought that this diagnosis was a blessing. The creativity was extraordinary, and the energy godlike, but most significant was the change in thought patterns. The unshakeable belief and optimism inevitably led to projects developing, and once projects began gaining traction, the momentum seemed to be relentless. The highs of a manic episode and particularly hypomania, which is the milder version of mania, whereby many people can function on a higher level, leave me feeling like I've tapped into a hidden chamber of human potential. If they could bottle hypomania, it would quickly become one of the most sought out drugs and probably lead to a significant increase in productivity. A drop in mood is never pleasant, but to see my mood drop from such an elevated level greatly amplified the pain. I'd pine for the hypomanic days of old as I'm sucked deeper and deeper into a black hole, where not even the smallest glimmer of light can escape. Those dark depressive days always felt like a curse.

Unfortunately, the foundation that these projects were built on was extremely volatile. With no warning, the rug would get pulled from under me, and the house of cards came tumbling down once depression hit.

Who was I trying to convince? And why was it so crucial that the diagnosis was incorrect? The narrative that I had formed internally had me as the victim in the story, battling the injustice dealt to me by the mental health institution. There was no room for any nuance in this position. And this led to the selective screening of information that fit this narrative. Time has proved to be the best healer; he has brought me perspective and most importantly, closure.

Ironically, I stopped taking medication to "feel like myself" again when in actuality, I feel most like myself now that I've resumed medication. The heights of mania and hypomania, as exhilarating as they are, come bundled with crippling periods of depression. My sense of sense gets buried somewhere between those two states. For me, bipolar disorder is neither a curse nor a blessing. This is a condition that I have to manage for the rest of my life. It's taken me almost five long years to get to this point, but I can finally say that I've made peace with the diagnosis. While the war may be over, the internal battle still rages on.

Integration

History has a funny way of repeating itself. Shortly after making peace with the diagnosis, side effects began to flare up due to the mood stabiliser that I was taking. The skin problems showed no sign of relenting, and I had to decide whether I wanted to continue this course of treatment, weighing up the risks and rewards of discontinuing the medication.

One of the better habits that I developed post-diagnosis was keeping track of my mood using a mobile application. I started making entries in 2018, but I used the app rather sporadically. Thanks to gamification, I began building up a streak of daily mood-tracking. Before I knew it, I had made 400 entries in a row — firmly establishing monitoring as part of my everyday routine. I had some robust data to work with, but I had never actually taken time to analyse the statistics. I found that my mood — since I began making entries — was good or better 75% of the time. It was a rather crude application of mathematics, but it was the most objective method I had at my disposal. Despite the lows of depression, I was managing very well. This data fed into a cost-benefit analysis, and ultimately, I came to a determination that the side effects were not worth it: the decision involved logic and faith. Faith that I can hold myself accountable and be open to reversing my decision if new evidence calls for it. I slowly weaned myself off the medication, and the skin problems cleared up after that.

If I were to move forward in life successfully, I would need to stop battling. Depression, mania, and my "true self" weren't three different entities. Accepting this, along with an understanding that mood fluctuations are inevitable, has allowed me to integrate the manic and depressive states. The extreme shifts in mood led to me living a fractured existence, and ultimately, I needed to experience a broken mind to be whole.

My return to spirituality was inevitable, but this time, I gravitated towards eastern philosophies, finding great wisdom in Buddhism. Alan Watts was my gateway drug. This time, however, my path wasn't undermined by religious dogma, and the teachings have helped build a firm foundation to draw upon, especially during periods of low mood. The deeper I dived into meditation, the more confident I felt about battling depression in the future.

Chapter Ten

THE ZONE OF DISCOMFORT

After four years at Richmond Upon Thames College, it was time for a new challenge. Senior managers had extinguished staff morale with a series of strange decisions. It was bittersweet and I didn't want to leave my first year students, but I had to put myself first for a change.

I was told about a vacancy at a college in Surrey. I browsed the website and was thoroughly impressed. It looked like an institution with sensible senior management. I put my soul into the application and the supporting statement. They invited me for an interview. As I sat down with the deputy headteacher, my thoughts changed from, *I would like to work in this college,* to *THIS IS THE PLACE FOR ME, I HAVE TO GET THIS POSITION.* I completed my 15-minute micro-teaching lesson and panel interview. The deputy headteacher uttered the dreaded words of 'We'll be in touch within the next few days.' How many times had I heard this only to be met with the '*Thank you for con-*

sidering this position but unfortunately...' email? Anxiety washed across my body. I had never wanted a position this badly. After 33 minutes, the train from Surrey arrived at Waterloo Station. I decided to walk home as it was a warm spring afternoon. My phone rang. It was a 0207 number. To my surprise, it was the deputy headteacher. I thought they would be calling in a few days as there were some more candidates to speak with. Maybe I misheard them. 'We would like to offer you the position to teach business at the college.' My entire being jumped for joy. I couldn't believe it. This was the closest thing to a dream job that I had encountered. I walked home with a giant smile plastered across my face.

I disclosed my bipolar disorder diagnosis and so would have to undergo medical clearance again. On a mild, May morning, I went to see a doctor in Kingston. I was dreading the process, particularly after what heaped at my last mental health screening which led to a three month delay in starting work at the college. However, and to my surprise, the entire process was painless. The doctor was warm and curious. I felt safe to explain what happened in 2015 and the events thereafter. Upon hearing the condensed version of my story, she told me that she thought I had been misdiagnosed and that it was not uncommon for a wrong diagnosis to happen.

The last day at college was emotional. I cried and was humbled by the gifts and the card that my colleagues gave me.

September 2022

The first six weeks of the academic year at my new college had zipped by with the names of new students now safely encoded into my long term memory. The only way I seemed to manage the workload and organisation necessary for a teacher was to wake up at 5 a.m. and get to work for 7 a.m. Watching a sea of faces squirm in disappointment at my half-baked lesson was a nightmare scenario that was always playing deep in the recesses of my mind.

October half term arrived. What would I do with all of this spare time? Teaching instilled a strong sense of purpose and now the 24 hours that the day afforded seemed burdensome. My sleep schedule was the first element of my daily routine to break. My thinking was that by waking up at 12 a.m., I would only have to survive another 12 hours before taking refuge under the duvet. Angst and anxiety coursed through my body. A sense of restlessness trickled down from limb to limb. The sense of unease reached fever pitch and I had to initiate the emergency protocol. Food. In times like this a subtle shift happens. It's as if 'Eché' slips into the passenger seat and an alter ego steps into the driver's seat.

I found myself at the local Tesco, watching helplessly as cakes, biscuits, muffins, and other calorific treats were added to the silver basket. Minutes passed and I was back in the flat ready to feast. The first thousand calories were nice but after the first pack of biscuits were dispatched, there was diminishing returns. That didn't stop the eating, though. Everything that was purchased was consumed there and then. Empty crisps and biscuit packets were strewn over the floor and before I knew it, my arms were violently opening kitchen cupboards in search of sweet and salty snacks. No luck. The next port of call would be food delivery apps. Burgers and fries were rapidly dispatched. I ate till it hurt. But at least I was feeling something. I christened days like this "McDonalds' days" two years ago. They tended to occur most during half terms and other school holidays.

I never learned to ride a bike during my formative years. And, ironically, the shame of not having learned prevented me from trying to learn as an adult. As a side effect, walking became my preferred mode of transport. I'd do so much more on foot. Inspired by the biography of David Goggins, I decided to really push myself and see how many steps I could take in a single day. At one point, 35,000 steps was my upper limit, then I managed to break into the 50,000 threshold. With continued training, I managed to hit 70,000 steps. That's when I decided that I would try to reach 100,000 steps. On a cold October morning, having slept over at a friend's house, I woke up around 4am and decided that today would be the day I'd pursue the 100k. I Walked from north to south and then from east to west. On my way, I encountered a myriad of rough sleepers plastered across London's streets, vulnerable to not only the elements but also the schemes of unruly pedestrians. It took me almost 17 hours but I managed to achieve 100,000 steps. It was only once I retired to my bedroom and took my shoes off that I felt the adrenaline wear off and sharp pains in my feet prevented me from sleeping soundly that evening.

Watching *Titanic* certainly made an impression on me. For all my life, I assumed a cruise was something only couples went on. As soon as I realised that solo cruises existed, I booked a northern European cruise courtesy of a 0% interest credit card. The defaults had finally lifted from my credit report and my rating was Excellent.

I arrived in Southampton and boarded the ship. The sheer magnitude of the vessel was striking. A true feat of engineering excellence. The cruise was like a moving hotel with every amenity one could ask for. You had the opportunity to craft whatever experience you wanted. There was a cinema, a theatre, dozens of restaurants, a gym, all kinds of swimming pools, and more. But despite all of the bells and whistles, I only went to the gym and ate at the same restaurant every day. My longest conversation was probably 'What floor are you going to?' whenever I found myself in the lift. I don't know if it was a conscious or unconscious decision, but for me, this cruise was certainly a retreat. This feeling of separation was compounded by the fact that I refused to pay £84 for the Wi-Fi on the ship. This meant that for half the trip, I had no internet access. It was only when we arrived at our destination that I would reconnect with the world. In the internet-less moments I found myself, for the first time in a long time, I was absolutely bored. I would sleep, meditate or read one of the Buddhism books that I'd brought with me. An extended morning meditation on the ship was an immediate habit. I wrote and explored my consciousness. I witnessed the strong desire for craving as I would over indulge in breakfast, lunch, and dinner. It wasn't as bad as the bingeing in London but I was much more aware of the sensation now that I was at sea.

We docked at Hamburg and I spent the afternoon walking around. It was cool, but what I was really waiting for was Rotterdam. That was the next stop. Shortly after the shop docked at Rotterdam, I was off to explore. I walked around sometimes guided by my GPS and other times, intuitively. Whilst using Google Maps to navigate, I noticed that there was a coffee shop nearby. Temptation swept over me. I had to try an edible. After failing to secure an edible at two coffee shops, I was successful in my third attempt. I was happy with my exploration and with the edible secured, I was ready to head back to the ship. On my way there, I noticed a shop advertising magic truffle seeds. Again, my curiosity was piqued and I stepped in. Just 10 metres into the shop to my right hand side was what I was quietly hoping to encounter. Truffles. They contained the same compound as magic mushrooms and I knew immediately that I would be making a purchase.

When I went to Amsterdam in 2022, I had tried a medium dose of truffles, only to be met with disappointment as nothing really happened. I was hoping for some visual distortion and a change of consciousness.

This time would be different. Instead of buying the medium dose I purchased the strongest truffle, rated 6/6 for strength. The man behind the counter asked if it was my first time. I told him no and completed the transaction.

Armed with both truffles and edibles, I was hopeful that I would finally open the doors of perception and hear the voice of God. The next day, I ate the truffle and waited, hoping to experience something similar to the many trip reports that I had listened to. No visual distortion. What I experienced wasn't a nightmarish trip, but it was overall an unpleasant one. Suddenly, my thought patterns were now anxious and I was powerless in responding to them with any effectiveness. I had to surrender to these thoughts and just accept this experience for what it was. The best way that I can describe it is being on a really bad roller coaster for five or six hours. I ended up lying in my bed waiting for the ordeal to be over. After washing away my disappointment, I began to contemplate. It soon dawned on me that my mental state prior to ingesting the truffles was much more preferable to its state upon ingestion. So, why on earth would I put myself through this again? For whatever reason, psilocybin didn't seem to do anything positive for me. At that moment, I decided that this would be the last time that I tried both truffles and edibles. *Everything is not for everybody,* I thought.

Chapter Eleven

CYCLES AND SPIRALS

The cruise only served to strengthen my passion for Buddhism. For the first time, morning meditations were now firmly established as a routine. I tried previously but always failed to maintain the consistency. I spent hundreds of pounds on dozens of Buddhist books and began attending group sessions at the London Buddhist Centre.

On my way home from a group mediation session, I ran into an old friend. Valentino was 6"5', dark skinned, and in Greek times, they would have carved statues out of reverence for his physique. We would train together, on and off, for about five years. During one of our last training sessions in 2016, he mentioned that whenever we would resume training after a few months hiatus, he wouldn't know which version of Eché to expect. I would either be lean and chiselled or suffering shin splints from carrying too much weight for my frame to painlessly hold.

For over 15 years, I have struggled with binge eating and I tried a myriad of strategies, from intermittent fasting to meditation. All without success. Perhaps I was asking the wrong question. Why did my weight fluctuate so dramatically? It was because I was obsessed with gaining muscle and so would eat excess calories in the hope of bulking up. Then, I would overdo the eating and would then have to eat in a calorie deficit to lose the excess weight. This yo-yo dieting pattern seemed inevitable. A new thought entered my consciousness: *What would happen if I stopped trying to bulk up? I am pretty content with my physique. What if I just trained, without the desire to get bigger.* My hypothesis was that if I stopped bulking then maintaining a healthy body weight would be much easier. The experiment was on. Months passed and I effortlessly maintained a lean frame. Crucially, I was able to do this through the winter, a time period that I typically struggle with weight management. Perhaps time will prove otherwise, but as far as I was concerned, this was the death of yo-yo dieting.

I continued to track my moods in order to understand and manage them. Each day, I would rate my mood on a 1-5 scale and list the activities that I engaged in on that particular day. I was then able to study the data and look for patterns. If my mood was continuously high, I would wonder whether I was experiencing hypomania (a milder form of mania). I had tracked my mood every day for almost four years. What I found in 2023 was that my mood was very stable and in five years of teaching, I had not taken any days off due to mental health. These two facts, along with my greater confidence in navigating depressed mood states, gave me the confidence to stop mood tracking altogether. The activity had been very useful but it's no longer necessary.

During a routine check-up with my doctor, I casually informed her that I was off the medication. She then removed the mood stabiliser, Lamotrigine, from my repeat prescription list. This moment was highly symbolic for me because at this point in my life, I know for a fact that I will never be taking mood stabilisers again.

Open-mindedness has always been my most dominant personality trait. It has taken me down some strange places and led to me adopting some *interesting* beliefs, but the same open mindedness that led me down the rabbit holes also enabled me to crawl my way back out.

A sudden feeling overcame me. My intuition was heightened and I felt connected to the source. I just knew what I had to do. It was a powerful, but familiar feeling. Suddenly, I had this urge to engage in spring cleaning. The sheer number of clothes, books, and other trinkets from the past that I held onto disgusted me. The laptop from 2015 had served me well but now it was time for a change. I had been working on a series of rap songs and wanted to properly record them. I also flirted with the idea of posting content on YouTube, so naturally, a new laptop was needed. I purchased a MacBook, but would give it to a friend after a few weeks of use. It was a great product but ultimately, not the right one for me. Instead, I purchased a desktop, on credit, which was more suited to my editing needs.

There was a pastor whose videos I used to watch back in 2016. He seemed to connect the dots and preached sermons that I never had heard before. His charisma and thorough research definitely spoke to me. He had passed away recently but the videos on his channel were still available. I clicked play and before I knew it, I was bingeing on hour long sermons. I stopped listening to music and would just absorb the insights. I was a Christian again, with the same zeal as in 2016. Feeling convicted by the pastor's sermons against secular music, I took my entire vinyl collection and threw it in the bin. I also ripped down my wallpaper which contained a collage of over 100 albums. I was all in. A hardcore, literalist, dogmatic Christian. As I continued to listen to these sermons, fear began to creep in. Suddenly, I lost direction and was second guessing myself. *Is this in line with the will of God?* I saw demons around every corner. *Is this salvation?* I thought. The notion of eternal hellfire cropped up and again, I struggled with it. I was giving indiscriminately to every person who held up a sign begging for money; even though I was broke and was using my credit card to withdraw the cash. Watching people give testimonies of going to hell increased the fear that I felt exponentially. I couldn't reconcile Buddhism and the Bible and so a decision needed to be made. I chose the Bible. I gathered up ten packets of incense and maybe 20 Buddhist books and threw them all in the bin. In this same state of mind, I decided to end the friendship with one of my best friends because it didn't seem compatible with my faith. All of this occurred within a span of fourteen days. I was ready to cut off any and everybody for the sake of Christianity.

One day, I left work early as I was not feeling too well. On my way back, I encountered five individuals with signs asking for money for a hostel. I gave every pound I could spare and then maxed out my credit card. On one hand, I thought that surely

God wanted me to help these people but then on the other hand, I wondered if God would want me to harm myself financially just to help these folks. My mind was fragile and could split at any moment. I was probably millimetres from a mental breakdown. Before going to bed that day, I prayed for God to bring clarity to my situation as God is surely not the author of confusion.

A few days later, as I stood in the kitchen washing the dishes, I began to think about my road to recovery. Buddhism had played an integral part in that journey. The meditation and four noble truths had certainly helped me navigate many moments of suffering. How could this be a demonic doctrine? More examples of the powerful lessons and tools that were now part of my arsenal flooded my mind. I was wrong. My literal interpretation of the Bible was the problem. I was a hardcore literalist Christian for about two weeks.

Interestingly enough, during the two-week spell, I felt disconnected from the source and from my intuition. However, as the days passed by and I began to explore gnostic and esoteric Christianity, I felt reconnected. This time, I wouldn't throw the baby out with the bathwater and abandon Christianity. Buddhist thinking and my interpretation of Christianity were wholly compatible.

I managed to prevent a crisis by controlling the energy. Unlike in 2015, I now had experience with this change in consciousness and was better prepared to handle it. By balancing my heart and rational mind, I was not only able to function but also operate at a very high level. I received a promotion at work, and the students were making wonderful progress. The album was very much on the horizon, and for the second time in my life, I felt alive.

This had the hallmarks of a 'manic episode,' but unlike eight years ago, I wasn't smoking high-grade skunk cannabis and taking antidepressants. An abundance of ideas would arrive, and I struggled to keep up with them. As I typed one idea, another would pop into my head. TikTok seemed almost tailor-made for me as I could quickly execute an idea and then move on to the next one. This effortless creativity led to writing and recording raps, and within a span of four months, I had completed 14 tracks while juggling a full-time teaching job and working on the very book you are reading. The same impulse to simplify my life led to clearing out my flat, but unlike in 2015, I didn't stop with possessions. I completely stopped consuming processed food; I wanted my diet to be as close to the Garden of Eden as possible. Discipline brings freedom. By deciding that my favourite snacks would no longer enter my house, navigating the supermarkets became very simple. There was no middle ground, and thus I had full freedom to operate within the parameters of my own rules.

The connection with my students was purer than ever because I see no distinction between them and my own kin. Now, being more present and conscious, I notice things that I previously did not see. For example, many of my students were creating self-fulfilling prophecies about never being able to grasp certain topics. How did I miss this before? I was now able to intervene and let them know that words create reality. My best lessons were delivered this academic year.

Do you believe in destiny? That perhaps a certain path has been laid out for you? Deep down, I know what I am supposed to do. Even though getting sectioned in 2015 threw me off course, a return to my life path was inevitable. The way my life has unfolded has made me believe that I have a divine destiny and that the suffering I experienced happened not to me, but for me. As I went down memory lane browsing social media posts, what I saw astounded me. In 2015, I set up a summer school; now, I am a teacher. Back then, I invested in a top-of-the-range computer so I could really focus on content creation. Again, history repeats itself, but this time, I purchased a PC. My heart's desire to empower and inspire a generation of young people has only been turbocharged. I feel compelled to create a political party and use it as the engine to bring awareness and help usher in fundamental, systematic change in Britain. The abolition of the monarchy is something that I envision will take place within a generation. Now, perhaps these are merely the delusions of a manic man who needs to be forcibly medicated. I guess time will tell.

Chapter Twelve

EPILOGUE

I continue to experience the same feeling from 2015, but this time without the negative effects. My sleep is sound and my thoughts certainly aren't racing anymore. I've stopped the weed, and antidepressants, and with these changes, I have greater mental clarity.

This experience has been profoundly transformative, and as cliche as it might sound, I wouldn't change a single aspect if I had the opportunity. All of the pain and suffering was essential and those experiences enabled me to integrate the aspects of my personality that I was repressing. Since being sectioned, I have experienced my most stable period of employment, a healthier relationship with food and fitness and most importantly, the ability to express myself and prevent emotions from bottling up. The fact that you are reading this book is a testament to this.

The road to recovery has been fraught with twists, turns, reversals, and relapse. I am grateful that I decided to keep driving, even where there was no sign of light at the end of the tunnel, and I had no idea where I was heading.

By going into the mental health hospital without my dentures I inadvertently confronted one of my biggest fears. Now I try to use fear as a compass and actively seek out areas in my life that are restricted by fear and steer aggressively in that direction.

Each day, I wake up hoping to be of service. In the West this experience is classed as a lifelong mental disorder. Perhaps if I was born elsewhere my experience would have been interpreted differently, and with more compassion.

I used to question the diagnosis. But that doesn't concern me as much. I don't identify with the label of bipolar disorder anymore. Now I am questioning the entire mental health framework that is used in the West. One of the British values that teachers have to preach to students, for the sake of OFSTED, is tolerance. So, why then, when it comes to matters of mental health, there is no tolerance for alternative frameworks? Spiritual experiences are chalked off as mere delusions.

Now that you have read my story, what framework do you think best describes my story; spiritual awakening or bipolar disorder?

Chapter Thirteen

ACKNOWLEDGEMENTS

I'm deeply grateful to everyone who has supported me along this journey, and I thank God for the suffering, the lessons, and for all the blessings bestowed upon me. To all the soul seekers out there, keep seeking, and remain relentless in your search until you connect with the source from which all things originate.

"The kingdom of God is within you" (Luke 17:21).

Disclaimer: This autobiographical novel is a sincere account of the author's life, based on their recollection of actual events. Every effort has been made to portray these events truthfully, as memory permits. While the core essence of the narrative is rooted in reality, it should be noted that, in some instances, dialogue has been supplemented for the sake of clarity and coherence. It is important to emphasize that all individuals portrayed within these pages are actual people, and no composite characters have been created. To protect their privacy and honour their wishes, the names of certain individuals have been altered. Furthermore, it is crucial to understand that this work does not provide any form of medical advice. Rather, it solely represents the author's personal story and experiences. Readers are encouraged to seek professional guidance for any medical or psychological concerns they may have.

ABOUT THE AUTHOR

Eche Egbuonu is an author, educator, and visionary on a mission to inspire and empower others through his words. With a deep passion for spirituality, personal growth, and social change, Eche weaves together his experiences, insights, and teachings to offer readers a transformative journey.

To learn more about Eche and explore his work, visit his website at www.echee.net. There, you'll find additional resources, articles, and updates on upcoming projects. Eche also invites you to connect with him on social media. Follow him on Tik Tok, Twitter and Instagram (@echeinlife) to stay in touch, share your thoughts on the book, and engage in meaningful conversations about spirituality, personal development, and societal transformation.

Don't hesitate to reach out and join the community of like-minded individuals who are seeking to connect with the source and make a positive impact on the world. Eche looks forward to hearing your insights and sharing this journey together.

To God be the Glory.

.

Printed in Great Britain
by Amazon